ISBN 978-1-332-15276-6
PIBN 10291756

This book is a reproduction of an important historical work. Forgotten Books uses state-of-the-art technology to digitally reconstruct the work, preserving the original format whilst repairing imperfections present in the aged copy. In rare cases, an imperfection in the original, such as a blemish or missing page, may be replicated in our edition. We do, however, repair the vast majority of imperfections successfully; any imperfections that remain are intentionally left to preserve the state of such historical works.

1 MONTH OF
FREE
READING

at

www.ForgottenBooks.com

By purchasing this book you are eligible for one month membership to ForgottenBooks.com, giving you unlimited access to our entire collection of over 700,000 titles via our web site and mobile apps.

To claim your free month visit:

www.forgottenbooks.com/free291756

English
Français
Deutsche
Italiano
Español
Português

www.forgottenbooks.com

Mythology Photography **Fiction**
Fishing Christianity **Art** Cooking
Essays Buddhism Freemasonry
Medicine **Biology** Music **Ancient**
Egypt Evolution Carpentry Physics
Dance Geology **Mathematics** Fitness
Shakespeare **Folklore** Yoga Marketing
Confidence Immortality Biographies
Poetry **Psychology** Witchcraft
Electronics Chemistry History **Law**
Accounting **Philosophy** Anthropology
Alchemy Drama Quantum Mechanics
Atheism Sexual Health **Ancient History**
Entrepreneurship Languages Sport
Paleontology Needlework Islam
Metaphysics Investment Archaeology
Parenting Statistics Criminology
Motivational

ouis the ourteenth

The Court of France
in the Seventeenth Century

By

Julia Pardoe

Volume IV

New York

ames Pott & Company

Mcmv

Savoy Edition

This edition is limited to Four Hundred
Copies of which this is
Number 2 0 8

List of Illustrations

CONTENTS OF VOL. IV

CHAPTER III

CHAPTER IV

Contents

CHAPTER VII

CHAPTER VIII

Contents

Contents

Louis XIV. and the Court of France in the Seventeenth Century

CHAPTER I

Louis XIV. and Mary de Mancini—Politic Lenity of Mazarin
—Mary de Mancini and Her Sister Removed from the Court
—Representation of the Œdipus of Corneille—Departure of
Mazarin for the Island of Pheasants—The Court Move to
the South—Disappointment of Mademoiselle d'Orleans—
Tedious Negotiations—The Marriage Contract—The Two
Diplomatists—Treaty of the Pyrenees—The Marshal of
Grammont at Madrid—Charles II. Solicits an Interview
with the Cardinal, and is Refused—Restoration of the
Prince de Condé to Favour—Death of the Duke of Orleans
—Extraordinary Conduct of Madame—The Abbé de Rancé
—The Head of Madame de Montbazon—Funeral of Mon-
sieur, and Conversion of the Abbé de Rancé.

THE gratification of the King at this unhoped-for
emancipation from a marriage which he had
considered as inevitable, was earnest and undisguised;
and the rather as, having been kept in ignorance of
the real progress of the negotiation with Spain, he believed that he was left free to indulge, for an indefinite
period, in his attachment to Mademoiselle de Man-

cini; and while the continued illness of Mazarin detained the Court at Paris, he amused himself in the
tennis-court, in drilling the musketeers, or in visiting
the Cardinal during the morning; and devoted the
remainder of the day to reading, or conversing with
Mary, with whom he also generally took his luncheon.
When the Queen retired for the night, he conducted
Mademoiselle de Mancini to her residence; contenting
himself at first by following in another carriage, or
driving the one she occupied; but ultimately, he
threw off even this restraint, and seated himself beside
her, profiting by the moonlight to drive for awhile in
the Place Bellecour.

So great was the liberty which she enjoyed, that
Mary at length began to feel seriously alarmed at the
studied neutrality of the Queen; and the more she reflected upon the circumstance the more she felt the
importance of clearing up a mystery, of whose existence her good sense sufficed to assure her. In this
difficulty she resolved to interrogate the Abbé Fouquet* upon the subject of the mysterious visitor whom
the Cardinal had received in disguise, and with whom
he had been closeted at midnight—never doubting
that this interview bore upon her present position.
The Abbé was, however, too cautious to betray the
secrets of his patron, and evasively replied that he was
one of those secret agents whom her uncle employed
in foreign Courts, and that he had been sent to inform
him that the Queen of Spain had given birth to a son.
Mary desired to hear no more; for in an instant the

* Abbé of Barbeaux and of Rigny, brother of Nicholas Fouquet,
the superintendent of finance.

effect of this unanticipated event became manifest to her. Philip IV., assured of a male successor to the throne, was now free to dispose of the hand of his daughter, and to seal, by these means, a peace between the two countries; she could not disguise from herself the desirableness of such a reconciliation to two nations exhausted by a long and harassing war, and she at once felt that all was lost. Meanwhile, Don Antonio Pimentelli, concealed in the apartments of the Cardinal, was engaged with him in preparing the different clauses of the treaty which was to secure the peace of Europe; but as nothing could be definitively arranged, save at a conference of the French and Spanish Ministers, an interview was at length arranged between Mazarin and Don Louis de Haro. The meeting was to be held on the frontiers of the two kingdoms, and it only remained to be decided on which side of the river it should take place.

After a short tour in the southern provinces, the Court returned to Paris; and still Mary de Mancini found herself treated with unlimited indulgence by the Queen, who, satisfied with the progress of the secret negotiations, felt convinced that a passion for an inferior, however violent, could not militate in the mind of Louis against the interests of his kingdom, and the gratification of receiving the hand of the first Princess in Europe. She had already forgotten her own youth, and the enthusiastic days when, wooed by the Duke of Buckingham, she had wept to remember that she was mated with a King.

The Court had not long been established once more in the Capital, and Mazarin was still occupied in discussing the various and conflicting claims of the two long-estranged nations, whose renewal of amity was to be effected by the gentle agency of a woman, ere he experienced a severe mortification, which he, however transmuted, with his usual ability, into a new source of personal honour. Several young noblemen had assembled, during the Holy Week, at Roissi, a chateau within a short distance of Paris; and there, while all classes of the population were engaged in the devotions imperative at so sacred a season, they abandoned themselves to the grossest dissipation—indulging in orgies so profane and disreputable that they soon became the subject of public comment.

Among them was the Marquis de Mancini, the nephew of the Cardinal, whose amiable qualities and personal advantages had greatly endeared him to the Court; and the rumour of the disorders in which he had been an actor no sooner reached the ears of Mazarin, than, refusing to listen to the entreaties in his favour, which were poured forth on all sides, he immediately banished him from the Capital; while he contented himself by simply remonstrating with his accomplices, who all belonged to the first families in the kingdom; and, after exhorting them to greater discretion in future, he dismissed them unpunished; by which means he conciliated the whole of the families of the young libertines, who, on witnessing his unrelenting severity towards a nephew to whom he was known to be deeply attached, had anticipated little mercy for those of their own blood.*

In like manner he sacrificed Mary to the exigencies

* Mémoires de Madame de Motteville.

of the Queen-mother, who represented to him that so long as she remained within reach of the King, who would resist every effort that might be made to deprive him of her society and counsel, they could entertain no hope either of a peace, or the alliance of which it was a condition. For a moment, however, the Cardinal hesitated; alleging that there was no reason to apprehend, should they act too suddenly, that the King might be roused to resistance; whereas, by proceeding calmly and gradually, and estranging the lovers almost imperceptibly, they might be enabled to carry their point without opposition.

An ironical smile played about the lips of Anne of Austria, as she remarked that the overmerciful policy lately adopted by his Eminence might, perhaps, fail to produce the effect which he appeared to anticipate; and that he would do well to reflect upon the nature of the advice which his niece was accustomed to bestow upon the King; and the great probability there existed that, if it were allowed time to work, it would soon emancipate Louis altogether from the authority of both his mother and his Minister.

The Queen was well aware of the force of this reflection upon the mind of the Cardinal, who dreaded nothing so much as the loss of power; and as she glanced towards him while pronouncing the remark, she saw, by the expression of his countenance, that she had struck home. He, nevertheless, affected to treat such a consideration lightly; and observed that the King was too well aware of the value of his services to dispense with them while they could be rendered available; upon which the Queen, forgetful of the restraint which she had hitherto put upon her suspicions, accused him of still nourishing unseemly hopes, based upon what he considered to be the weakness of his Sovereign; and renewed her declaration that she would sooner die than see her son commit the infamy of a marriage by which he must be degraded.*

Stung by the expression, Mazarin was about to withdraw; when the Queen, instantly conscious of the error she had committed, prevented his purpose, and conjured him to overlook a few hasty words wrung from her in the excitement of a moment in which she felt that all her dearest interests were at stake; upon which, with his usual policy, he smiled away the insult he was never likely to forget, and declared that, in or-der to prove to her Majesty how greatly she had wronged him by her suspicions, he would at once re-move both Mary and her sisters to his chateau at Brouage.†

Having come to this resolution, he lost no time in summoning Madame de Venelle, the governess of Hortensia and Mary Anne de Mancini; and, after having directed her to watch all Mary's movements, gave her orders to prepare her charges for an immediate removal to Brouage. Louis, however, no sooner heard of the arrangement than he hastened to demand an

---

* Mémoires de Madame de Motteville.

† Brouage is a fortified seaport town in the department of the Lesser Charente, opposite the island of Oléron. It was founded in 1555 by James, Lord of Pons, and fortified during the religious wars. After the taking of La Rochelle, Richelieu renewed the fortifications, and erected it into a government, he being himself the first Governor. It possessed an excellent harbour, which, in the 17th century, was blocked with mud. The environs of Brouage are covered by un-wholesome marshes, and the finest salt works in France are found there.

explanation of the Cardinal, and refused to permit the departure of Mademoiselle de Mancini from the Court. Vainly did the Minister represent the probable disgust of the Infanta, should she learn that, even while the negotiations of marriage were pending, the King retained near him a person to whom his attachment had long ceased to be problematical, the indignation of Philip IV., and the consequent continuance of a war which was rapidly exhausting the resources of the kingdom. Louis declared his determination not to sacrifice his personal happiness to such considerations; alleging that France was quite able to protect itself against Spain as it had hitherto done; that the war would afford him opportunities of convincing his people that he was worthy to be their Sovereign; and that rather than be the cause of unhappiness to Mary, he was willing and anxious to raise her to the throne—an event which must secure to the Cardinal a fixed and honourable position, of which no national disaffection could thenceforth deprive him.

Mazarin shook his head coldly and incredulously. "That person," he said, "has no regard for me; but, on the contrary, a vast deal of aversion, because I do not encourage her in her madness. Her ambition is beyond all bounds, and her spirit warped and violent. She despises every one, throws off all restraint, and is always ready to commit a thousand extravagances. It is believed that I have secretly encouraged her, and this reflection overwhelms me. I neither eat nor sleep, and am wasting away with vexation and uneasiness. If things last much longer in this state, I will embark with all my family, and go and hide myself in some corner of Italy, where we shall never be heard of again." *

A few violent words did not, however, suffice to dissuade the young Sovereign from his purpose; and he reiterated his resolution to marry Mary, and thus place her beyond the power of her enemies; but the Cardinal remained firm; and although Louis wept, and, as some authors affirm, even knelt before the inexorable Minister, to induce him to recall his verdict, he did so without effect. For an instant the indignant King even contemplated opposition; but as Mazarin, who had never for a moment laid aside his attitude of command, continued to expatiate upon the miseries to which his obstinacy upon this subject would expose, not only the Court but the whole kingdom, the unhappy young Monarch, painfully conscious of his utter helplessness, and terrified by so fearful a prophecy, threw himself into a chair, and burying his face in his hands, fell into a stupor of despair.

The Cardinal felt that he had conquered; and he had, indeed, obtained a double victory, over his own ambition, and the first serious affection which Louis had ever experienced. The departure of Mary was consequently decided on; and upon the previous evening the King paid his usual visit to the Queen-mother in a state of wretchedness which he made no effort to conceal. He had no sooner entered her apartment than Anne of Austria, taking a flambeau from the table, retired with him to the bath-room, where they were closeted together for an hour, and on their reappearance both were evidently affected; the eyes of the

* Extract from a MS. collection of Letters written at Libourne.

King were red with weeping, and in a few moments he withdrew.*

The dreaded morrow arrived; and when the nieces of the Cardinal had taken leave of the Queen, Mary proceeded to the King's apartment, where she found him deluged in tears.

"Sire," she exclaimed, reproachfully, as, with a dry eye and a quivering lip, she approached his chair, and extended towards him her trembling hand, "you are a King—you weep—and yet I go!"

The only reply of Louis was a fresh burst of sorrow, as he suffered his head to fall upon the table, without the utterance of a syllable. But Mary needed no other answer. She at once felt that all was over between them; and her pride enabled her to withdraw from his presence without one attempt at reproach or expostulation. Her sisters were already seated in the carriage, and she took her place beside them, scarcely appearing to remark that she had been followed by the King, who remained standing upon the same spot until the carriage had disappeared, when he departed for Chantilly, in order to indulge his grief in solitude.

During this time the veteran Corneille had produced his Œdipus, and Molière was pursuing his representations at the theatre of the Petit-Bourbon. Moreover, two other celebrities had appeared, although they were yet to acquire the undying fame which awaited them hereafter; one was La Fontaine, who at this period took up his abode at Paris; and the other, Bossuet; while Racine and Boileau began to give the promise of

* Mémoires de Madame de Motteville.

future excellence which their after career so fully
realised.

Four days after the departure of his nieces the Cardinal left Paris in his turn, with a princely retinue, for
the Island of Pheasants,* which had been ultimately
decided on as the rendezvous of the contracting parties for the royal marriage. In his suite he had two
Archbishops, four Bishops, three Marshals, and several nobles of the highest rank; as well as M. de
Lyonne, the Minister of State, who was to assist him
in his labours. Don Antonio Pimentelli had already
preceded him, to announce his approach to the Spanish
Minister; while, on the day of his arrival at St. Jean
de Luz, the Court left Fontainebleau for the south,
although it was not generally known that the King
had absolutely refused to undertake this journey until
it had been conceded that in passing Cognac he should
have an interview with Mary de Mancini. The arguments of the Queen against this measure were at first
vehement; but as Louis persisted in his purpose, it was
ultimately arranged that the meeting should take place.

Great preparations were made by all those who had
been selected to accompany the Court; and the most
magnificent apparel was prepared, in order to do honour to the royal nuptials; while as the illustrious *cortège*
passed along the streets of Paris, the acclamations of
the populace were loud and long; and a thousand
blessings were called down upon the head of the young
King, and a thousand prayers put up for the success
and safety of his journey.

* The Island of Pheasants is a small Spanish islet formed by the
Bidassoa, within a league of Fontarabia and the Gulf of Gascony.

The Queen-mother was accompanied by the Princess of Conti ; the Princess-Palatine ; the Countess of Flex, her lady of honour ; and the Duchess of Uzès. From Fontainebleau, the Court first proceeded to Chambord, where *Monsieur* and *Madame* were then residing for a few days ; and upon the road the King gayly remarked to MADEMOISELLE, who was also in the Queen's coach, that he had not changed his dress nor untied his hair, because he apprehended that by increasing his good looks he should heighten the regret of his uncle, as well as that of *Madame*, and Mademoiselle d'Orleans, her sister, who had long been taught to consider herself as his future wife ; and that he had consequently disfigured himself as much as possible. Nor had *Monsieur* and *Madame* been wholly without misgivings on their side. *Madame* being not only mortified at the failure of a marriage with her daughter, of which she had so long contemplated the possibility, that she had finally considered it as certain ; but also tormented with fearful visions of the outlay which would be necessitated by the Royal visit ; to which she had only become tolerably reconciled by the almost daily letters of MADEMOISELLE, which, in all probability, contained something more weighty than mere argument.

The uneasiness of *Monsieur*, although less squalid, was scarcely less puerile and undignified. He had amused himself since his sojourn at Blois by preserving pheasants, of which he possessed immense numbers, and which he never suffered to be destroyed ; and the conviction that the King would not omit to profit by so excellent an opportunity of enjoying a favourite sport, made him perfectly wretched.

When the Court arrived at Blois, Mesdemoiselles
d'Orleans and de Valois received their Royal relatives
at the foot of the stairs, attended by their scanty train
of ladies; and although each individual had made immense exertion to present a favourable appearance, the
antiquated air of their costume afforded legitimate subject for merriment among the more modish attendants
of the Queen.

As he alighted, the King complimented *Madame* on
the beauty of his cousin, Mademoiselle d'Orleans;
whom, however, he saw at an unfortunate moment,
her mortification upon hearing that he was about to
form an alliance with the Infanta being legibly impressed upon her countenance; which, coupled with
the fact that she was extremely disfigured by the
bites of some gnats that had stung her during the
night, robbed her of her brilliant complexion which is
the greatest charm of youth. When the party had
entered the palace, the courtiers dispersed themselves
through the apartments and galleries, criticising aloud
the superannuated appearance of the furniture, and the
obsolete dresses of the ladies; nor were they more
conciliating during the dinner, of which they affected
to be afraid to partake; while MADEMOISELLE sat by,
trembling with mortification and annoyance.* Neither
the King nor his mother disguised their anxiety to be
gone; and they were no sooner again upon the road
than they indulged in numerous mirthful reminiscen-
ces of their visit, which were gall and wormwood to
the haughty spirit of MADEMOISELLE; who was, nevertheless, compelled to smile when Louis described to

* Mémoires de Madame de la Vallière.

her the evident discomposure of her father at the destruction of the fourteen pheasants which he had killed while awaiting dinner.

It was with an aching heart that Mademoiselle de Mancini had received an order from the Queen to proceed with her sisters to St. Jean d' Angély, to await the passage of the Court, in order to pay their respects to her Majesty ; for the fact that the Queen had herself commanded this meeting sufficed to assure Mary that she no longer dreaded her influence; and the idea of again seeing the King, only to look on him in the midst of a crowd of courtiers, tortured her almost beyond endurance. Proud in her own integrity, she nevertheless made a powerful effort to suppress all exhibition of her wretchedness, and entered the presence of the Queen with a calm dignity which astonished all around her.

Her interview with the King was, however, a bitter one; for, divided between vanity and affection, Louis was at once less firm and less self-possessed than Mary. He wept bitterly, and bewailed the fetters by which he was shackled; but, as he remarked the change which nights of watching and of tears had made in her appearance, he felt half consoled; and the only result of this meeting was to harrow the heart of the poor victim of political expediency, and to prove to her upon how unstable a foundation she had blindly built up her superstructure of hope.

From St. Jean d'Angély the Court proceeded to Bordeaux, and thence to Toulouse, where they halted to await the conclusion of the treaty. The negotiation was a tedious one. The pardon of the Prince de

Conde, and his restoration to all his honours, was a point which the Cardinal was long in conceding; and this was no sooner arranged than fresh difficulties arose as to every city which was to be claimed or ceded. Weakened as he was in health, not only by the disease from which he was suffering, but also from the immense fatigue and want of rest which he was compelled to undergo, Mazarin nevertheless rallied all his energies, and refused to ratify the treaty until he had rendered it one of unequivocal advantage to the nation which he represented. It was then signed by both Ministers in duplicate; after which they also appended their signatures to the marriage contract.

This contract insured to the Infanta a portion of five hundred thousand golden crowns, payable in three instalments; in consideration of which sum she formally renounced " all other pretensions to the inheritance of her parents, it being clearly understood that neither she nor her children could succeed to any of the states of his Catholic Majesty, even in the event of his legitimate successors becoming extinct."

The Marshal of Grammont, who had only awaited the signing of the treaty, then took leave of their Majesties, and hastened as Ambassador-Extraordinary to Madrid, to demand the hand of the Infanta; while the Cardinal, worn out both in body and mind, arrived at Toulouse, after a three months' sojourn in the unwholesome air of the Island of Pheasants. Between the two Ministers the whole of the arrangements, as well as the treaty itself, had been one great diplomatic struggle; for although the marriage of the King and the general peace of Europe were the objects of the conference, more than a month was spent in settling the difficulties of precedence, and in regulating the ceremonies to be observed. The Cardinals placed themselves on an equality with crowned heads, and France claimed preeminence over the other European powers; but Don Louis de Haro would concede neither of these assumptions, and refused to treat save on equal terms, both as regarded himself and the nation of which he was the representative. Mazarin brought to the strife all his usual dexterity and cunning; and Don Louis a slowness and deliberation which afforded him ample time to sift the policy of his opponent to the very dregs, although he refrained from offering any pledges, or holding out any promises; while the Cardinal was lavish of both, although they were all equivocal. The aim of the Italian was to take his antagonist by surprise, that of the Spaniard to guard himself from an attempt which he had soon penetrated; and it was asserted that the latter had remarked of the Cardinal, that his policy was very mistaken upon one point, for he was always seeking to deceive.

Be that as it might, it is certain that, save as regarded the peace, Mazarin obtained no actual advantage through this marriage. The portion of Maria Theresa which, as we have already stated, was nominally fixed at five hundred thousand gold crowns, would not, had it been forthwith paid into the treasury, have covered the outlay of the King's journey to the frontier to receive her. Nevertheless, these five hundred thousand crowns, equal at that period to two millions five hundred thousand livres, were a great subject of contestation between the Ministers; and finally, France never received more of the dower than a hundred thousand francs.

Charles IV., Duke of Lorraine, was, by this treaty, made to feel the vengeance of both the kingdoms against which he had borne arms; and he was sacrificed by each the more readily that he was no longer in a position to oppose their united verdict. France restored to him his principality, but demolished Nancy, and placed an interdict upon his maintaining armed troops; while, in the case of the Prince de Condé, against whom Louis XIV. had even greater cause of complaint, Don Louis de Haro obliged the Cardinal to give a pledge of his restoration to the favour of his Monarch, by a threat that, should this article be rejected, Spain would continue to him the sovereignty of Rocroy, Câtelet, and other fortresses of which he was then in possession. By her concession upon this point, France consequently gained, not only the renewed fealty of her greatest general, but also the cities just named.*

Both these subtile Ministers were, however, guilty of one act of policy, as short-sighted as it was contemptible. Charles II., at that period hopeless of regaining his throne through his own efforts, or those of his immediate friends, who had already fruitlessly exhausted both their blood and their resources in his cause, no sooner heard of the conference of the Pyrenees than he hastened to implore the help of Don Louis and Mazarin, flattering himself that their respective Sovereigns, who were both his relatives, would, at last, upon

* Le Siècle de Louis XIV. *Francheville.*

the occasion of their alliance—Cromwell, moreover, being dead—revenge a cause in which all the crowned heads of Europe were individually interested; but neither Don Louis nor the Cardinal would concede an interview to the unhappy and exiled King, fearing to rouse the resentment of the English ambassador, who was still at St. Jean de Luz.

Could Charles have foreseen that only a few weeks were destined to elapse ere he should be summoned by his own subjects to assume his birthright, and to ascend the throne of his ancestors, without one helping hand from among the mighty potentates of Europe, he might have spared himself that last and useless humiliation. Certain it is that this unlooked-for event occurred so suddenly that he was in peaceful possession of his kingdom before the treaty of the Pyrenees was signed.

The reception of the Marshal of Grammont at Madrid had, meanwhile, been most triumphant. He had entered the city post, in order to testify the impatience of his master, magnificently attired in the garb of a courier, and followed by a splendid retinue; * and, on his arrival, the Admiral of Castille had invited him to a gorgeous banquet; which, however, like the feast of the Barmecide, was meant rather for the eye than for the palate. Seven hundred dishes, emblazoned with the arms of the Admiral were served up, of which the contents were covered with saffron and

* " The Marshal of Grammont left this city for St. Jean de Luz, and thence for Madrid, not only with the most attractive retinue, but also with an immense suite of persons of distinction, who were anxious to increase the splendour of an embassy of this importance."—*Bayonne Gazette of the 27th Sept., 1659.*

gilding; but all were in succession carried away untouched, to the great discomfort of the guests, who were compelled to sit for four hours spectators of these unprofitable evolutions.*

The fêtes and galas given by the King of Spain, in honour of his arrival, revenged him, however, on the visionary banquet of the Admiral, and left no doubt of the success of his mission.

As the Court left Toulouse M. de Condé quitted Brussels, accompanied by his wife, his daughter, and his son; and at Coulommeirs he was met by the Duke and Duchess of Longueville; when, after a hasty greeting, the former went forward to announce his approach to the Court, where the Prince de Conti had already arrived. Two days afterwards Condé reached Aix in his turn; and when he was announced to the Queen, MADEMOISELLE was in the apartment of her Majesty, awaiting with anxiety the appearance of the illustrious rebel; but she was fated, for the present, to disappointment, as Anne of Austria had no sooner ascertained the identity of her visitor than she turned to the Princess, and requested her to leave the room, asserting that M. de Condé had desired that their first meeting might take place without witnesses. MADEMOISELLE replied with a bitter smile that she was convinced the Prince would consider her absence upon such an occasion very extraordinary. The Queen, however, retorted in an angry tone, and MADEMOISELLE found herself compelled to obey, which she did with an ill grace; and proceeded forthwith to complain to the Cardinal of the want of consideration which

* Memoires du Maréchal de Grammont.

had been shown to her, declaring that, should she be subjected to a renewed affront of this nature, she would immediately withdraw from Court. Mazarin made an ample apology, by which the haughty Princess was appeased; and M. de Condé, having shortly afterwards paid her a visit, she soon forgot her momentary mortification.*

The Prince, meanwhile, relieved every one about him of the embarrassment which might have been felt upon the occasion of his reappearance, by the perfect self-possession which he exhibited, and by accosting each individual with whom he came in contact with the easy and indifferent air of one who had only parted from them the previous evening; and he had not been many hours in Aix ere the King was talking familiarly to him of all that he had accomplished both in France and Flanders, with as much interest as though he had performed all these exploits in the Royal Service.

On the evening succeeding the departure of the Court for Toulon, as MADEMOISELLE was writing in her apartment, a courier from Blois was announced, who proved to be a jester on the establishment of *Monsieur*, and who threw upon her table a large packet of papers, exclaiming that her father was not dead, nor did he believe that he was likely to die this time; and then, without explaining the meaning of this extraordinary announcement, asked if the Cardinal were in the city, as he had a letter to deliver to him.

The Princess, greatly alarmed, inquired into the motive of his journey; when he stated that *Monsieur*

* Mémoires de Mademoiselle de Montpensier.

had been suffering from brain-fever, but that he was now better; and that his object was to inform the Court of the circumstance. The letters of MADEMOISELLE, however, gave a less favourable opinion of the temporary convalescence of her father; and the certificate of the physicians, by which they were accompanied, left no doubt of the gravity of the attack, nor of their apprehensions as to the result which might supervene.

Under these circumstances, the Princess lost no time in sending a messenger to the Cardinal, stating her anxiety to start immediately for Blois; but Mazarin declared that he was not aware if her departure would be strictly according to etiquette, and that she must delay her purpose until he ascertained the fact. In obedience to this decision, MADEMOISELLE contented herself by ordering prayers to be put up in all the churches, and awaited, as patiently as she could, the permission of the Court to assist in closing the eyes of her dying father. On returning from the evening service of the Fathers of the Oratory on the following Sunday, she found all her retinue assembled in her antechamber; and the truth flashed upon her at once —*Monsieur* was dead; and retiring to her closet she burst into tears.

MADEMOISELLE could not, however, even while she wept as a daughter, forget that she was also a Princess; and, accordingly, she soon sufficiently controlled her filial emotion to remember that it was her duty to inform the King of the death of his uncle. " These are dignified proceedings," she remarks, " in which we should never fail." She, therefore, sustained by this reflection, dried her tears, and wrote a letter to the

Cardinal, informing him that her grief would not allow her to address the King; but that as her duty obliged her to inform his Majesty of the death of *Monsieur*, she requested him to perform the office for her. She then sent a gentleman to wait upon the Queen and the Duke of Anjou with the melancholy tidings, and proceeded to write a second letter to the Prince de Conti, to inform him of her anxiety that he should succeed to the government of Languedoc, for which she strongly advised him to apply; but counselled him, at the same time, not to speak of any private government, in order that all such might be left to those upon whom *Monsieur* had himself bestowed them; after which she gave the necessary orders for her mourning, and then retired to rest, " occupied by a sincere regret at the death of *Monsieur*."

We have shown how MADEMOISELLE bore the loss of her last parent; let us now turn to the little Court of Blois, and examine the effect produced by the demise of Gaston upon those by whom he was immediately surrounded.

Madame was not present when he expired; but he no sooner ceased to breathe than she demanded the keys of the presses, in which she locked up the dinner-services, the plate, and everything that came under her hand; and having secured all articles of value, she discharged the whole of her household, retaining only a few Lorrainese attendants, who were as rapacious as herself. She next removed the sheets from the bed upon which *Monsieur* lay dead; and as there was, consequently, no linen left in which to shroud the corpse, it became necessary for some one to supply it;

when Madame de Rare, the governess of his daughters, gave the last proof of her attachment to her master by furnishing the death-sheet in which he was carried to his grave.* Moreover, the usual religious ceremonies were neglected, and scarcely a prayer was said for the son, the brother, and the uncle of three powerful sovereigns. The doors of the apartment in which he lay were closed every evening, and the priests left the body unattended during the night. Notwithstanding the severity of the cold, neither light nor fire was allowed in the room ; and when, after having laid in state for several days, the body was finally removed to St. Denis, the funeral procession was composed only of a few pages and almoners.

Etiquette prescribed for *Madame* a retirement of forty days in an apartment hung with black, where she should have received the condolences of the public bodies, and of her own private friends ; but Marguerite of Lorraine was not, as we have shown, a person to be influenced by common rules ; and, although no Princess had yet ventured to neglect this last ceremonial of mourning, she dispensed with the restraint and the expense alike, and at the end of eleven or twelve days reappeared in the midst of her diminished household, to the great scandal of all its members. Nor was this all ; for, having arranged her affairs at Blois, she announced her intention of forthwith proceeding to Paris, to entreat the King in behalf of herself and her

---

* It is a singular fact that a similar circumstance occurred at the death of *Madame* herself. After her body had been embalmed not one of her women would give a chemise for her to be buried in, but said that they did not possess any ; and it was the Princess of Wirtemberg who supplied the linen necessary for her decent interment.

daughters; and when she set forth for this purpose, instead of travelling in a close coach, she selected an open carriage, by which means she was recognised in every town and village through which she passed.*

The curate of St. Saviour of Blois had attended the Prince in his last moments, the principal of the Oratory, who was his confessor, not being upon the spot, while the Abbé de Rancé,† the nephew of the Archbishop of Tours, attached himself with exemplary devotion to his Royal Highness, and, until he expired, remained constantly by his bedside.

Previously to that period he had been known only by his companionable qualities, his powers of intellect, and his utter disregard of the duties of his sacred profession; but the deathbed of *Monsieur*, as MADEMOISELLE relates, changed the whole tenor of his life. Conscious of the errors of his past career, beside the body of the almost forsaken Prince, whose passage to the tomb he had so materially assisted to render happy, he formed the resolution of abandoning a world by which he had been so grievously misguided; and as he had the control of the Abbey of la Trappe, he at once determined that it should be the place of his penance, for which purpose he requested permission of the King to reform the community, and had no sooner received the Royal sanction to that effect than he took the vows of the rigid order of St. Benard, and was deputed by the whole body to proceed to Rome, where he succeeded admirably in his mission, and displayed so much piety

---

* Mémoires de Madame de la Vallière.

† Dom Armand John le Bouthillier, nephew of the superintendent of finance.

and ability that he was soon regarded as a worthy successor to the saint whose garb he wore.   On his return to France he reorganised his abbey, and placed it
upon the same footing which it held in the time of its
holy founder.

Other authorities, however, attribute the conversion
of M. de Rancé to a very different cause.   The whole
of his youth had been devoted to dissipation; and ·
among other women of rank to whom he had attached
himself in a manner unbecoming his profession, was
the beautiful but dissipated Duchess of Montbazon,
from whom, on one occasion, he had been compelled
to separate himself for a short time, and to whose
residence he hastened immediately on his return from
his journey, ignorant that she had died during his absence.   Entering her apartment unannounced, he was
horror-struck on seeing her head placed upright upon
a dish, the leaden coffin which had been prepared having been found too short for the body; and this sight,
for which he had been totally unprepared, produced so
great an effect upon his mind, that it determined him
to the retreat which has been already mentioned! *

Certain it is that this conversion created infinitely
more sensation than the death by which it had been
preceded, for Gaston left scarcely a regret behind him.
Always disaffected and suspicious, he was perpetually
in a state of moral revolt; and when circumstances
occasionally compelled him to put his theories into
practice, he unhesitatingly sacrificed all those who had
been weak enough to trust to his honour, when by such
measures he could insure his own safety.   Not one of

* Dictionnaire Encyclopédique de Charles Saint-Laurent.

all his friends escaped some share of suffering for his sake: exile, imprisonment, and death had been alike the reward of their misplaced confidence in his principles; and his abandonment of their interests in the hour of need was so notorious, that, on one occasion, when at a public rejoicing, he extended his hand to the Prince de Guémenée, who had ascended some steps, the Prince said, with a somewhat equivocal smile, " I thank your Royal Highness the more sincerely for your help, as I am the first of your friends whom you ever assisted to descend from a scaffold:" * a bitter pleasantry, which must have smitten with momentary shame even Gaston of Orleans.

Neither the death of a member of the Royal House, nor the conversion of an abbé of the Court, were, however, events of sufficient importance to divert the thoughts of all classes for more than a very brief interval from the approaching marriage of the King; and, accordingly, Gaston was laid beside his illustrious kindred in the gloomy vaults of St. Denis, and the iron gates closed behind him, never again to revolve upon their hinges until they once more fell back to admit another inmate to this Necropolis of departed royalty, while De Rancé buried himself in the living tomb of La Trappe, to fast and pray, exist in eternal silence, and daily dig his grave with his own hands, without leaving any lasting impression upon the public mind.

Every eye was turned towards the Pyrenees.

* Louis XIV. et son Siècle.

CHAPTER II

CONSIDERABLE surprise was felt by the Court when they received an intimation that the marriage of the Sovereign was postponed until the following spring; the severity of the weather, and the consequent probability of a rigorous winter, being a pretext for this delay on the part of the King of Spain, who could not, as he asserted, expose himself without imprudence, at such a season, to a journey for which both his age and his infirmities unfitted him.

In the interval which consequently elapsed, intelligence reached the French Court of the death of the second Prince of Spain, and great alarm was felt both by the Queen and Mazarin that this event would prevent the completion of the treaty; but, as peace had become quite as desirable for the one kingdom as for the other, their fears were not realised; and in the month of May, 1660, Louis XIV. and his Court left Toulouse for Bayonne, and thence proceeded to St. Jean de Luz, where they were to be met by the King of Spain and the Infanta.

Nothing could exceed the magnificence of the preparations for this royal and nuptial interview. A temporary palace had been erected in the Isle of Pheasants, which was redolent of Spanish splendour and French elegance; a bridge connected the island with the mainland on either frontier; and infinite difficulties had been vanquished in order to place the two Sovereigns on a perfect equality, even in the most minute details of accommodation and ornament. The bridges, forming covered galleries, were precisely similar, and led to two saloons splendidly furnished and decorated, having lateral chambers and dressing-rooms; while in the exact centre, calculated to an inch of surface, was the grand hall of meeting, which was extremely spacious, and lighted only on the riverward side. Two doors of entrance, placed precisely opposite to each other, enabled the two great contracting parties to make a simultaneous entrance; while the floor, divided in a straight line across the centre, was covered on the Spanish side with Persian carpets wrought on a ground of gold and silver; and the moiety which belonged to France was overspread with crimson Genoa velvet, laced with gold and silver. In each compartment were placed an armchair and a table; and upon the latter stood two inkstands and two timepieces; in short, not the slightest deviation, save in the material which covered the floor, was perceptible in the respective sides of the vast apartment.*

On the 3d of June, Don Louis de Haro, as the proxy of Louis XIV., having the Bishop of Fréjus as his witness, married the Infanta Maria-Theresa, daughter of Philip IV., King of Spain, in the church of Fontarabia, where the ceremony was conducted with the most stately and chilling gravity. MADEMOISELLE, who had with some difficulty obtained permission to attend the espousals *incognita*, relates that a dais of gold brocade, inclosed by curtains save on the side next the altar, had been prepared for the King in the tribune, and beside it was placed a seat for Don Louis de Haro, with, beyond this, a bench for the grandees of the kingdom on one side, and a second for the almoners directly opposite. All the French who were present occupied the steps of the altar.

The King entered the Church, preceded by a few Swiss guards, the larger portion of the troops remaining at the entrance ; and immediately before him walked the Bishop of Pampeluna, with the whole of his clergy, in full sacerdotal costume. Philip IV. wore a grey coat embroidered with silver, and his hat looped with a large diamond, to which was attached a pendent pearl, both belonging to the crown jewels. He was followed by the Infanta, who walked alone, dressed in white satin, richly embroidered, and ornamented with small bows of silver serge, a quantity of ill-set gems, and a mass of false hair. Her train was carried by her first lady of the household.†

* Mémoires de Mademoiselle de Montpensier.
† *Cameriéri Major* are persons who, in the Peninsular Courts, have

By some strange oversight, the Bishop of Fréjus was not apprised of the precise hour at which the marriage had been appointed to take place; and the service was actually about to commence when he was missed, and a messenger hastily despatched to his residence, whence he arrived without delay totally unattended; and with evident chagrin reproached Don Louis for his neglect, as he passed on to take his place at the altar.

At the conclusion of the mass, Philip IV. seated himself in his chair of state, and the Infanta took her place upon her cushion; after which the Bishop also seated himself, and Don Louis approached, and presented to him the procuration of the King of France, which the Bishop of Fréjus had just delivered into his hands. It was read by one of the assistant priests, as were also the Papal dispensations; after which the marriage service was performed; the King standing the whole time between the Infanta and Don Louis.

When the Princess was called upon to make her affirmative reply, she turned round and faced her father, making, when she had so done, a very profound curtsey, as if to solicit his permission to utter it, which was apparently conceded; she then slowly and gravely moved her lips, and answered in a low, firm tone. Throughout the whole of the ceremony, the Infanta never once gave her hand to Don Louis, nor did he present the ring to her. At the termination of the service she knelt before the King, and kissed his hand; after which Philip withdrew his hat, and embraced

unlimited authority over the servants of the palace; dress and undress the King, or other member of the Royal family whom they serve, and exercise their jurisdiction over all which relates to the internal economy of the household.

her. She then rose, placed herself on the King's right hand, and the whole train swept after them from the church.

Nothing could more thoroughly illustrate the different genius of the two nations than the manner in which they observed the Royal marriage day. At Fontarabia not a vestige of rejoicing was to be detected; all was grave, and still, and monotonous as usual; while in France the people were profuse in outlay both of money and acclamation. Their joy amounted, indeed, almost to delirium.*

"The Infanta," says Madame de Motteville, who accompanied MADEMOISELLE to witness the marriage, "is short, but well made; we admired the extreme fairness of her complexion; her blue eyes appeared to us to be fine, and charmed us by their softness and brilliancy. We celebrated the beauty of her mouth, and of her somewhat full and roseate lips. The outline of her face is long, but being rounded at the chin, pleased us; her cheeks, rather large but handsome, had their share of our praise; her hair, of a very light auburn, accorded admirably with her fine complexion. To speak the truth, with more height, and handsomer teeth, she would deserve to be estimated as one of the most beautiful persons in Europe. Her bust appeared to be well formed and tolerably full; but her dress was horrible." †

On the following day, Anne of Austria, the King of Spain, and the royal bride met on the Island of Conference. The Queen-mother arrived first, Philip

---

* Louis XIV., sa Cour, et le Regent.
† Mémoires de Madame de Motteville.

IV. having been detained at Fontarabia by the visit of the Duke of Créqui, who waited upon him in the name of his Royal master, to present to the young Queen, not the jewels of the crown, but those which Louis offered as his marriage gift, and which were very fine. She was accompanied only by *Monsieur* (the Duke of Anjou, now Duke of Orleans), etiquette not permitting the young King to have an interview with his bride before a given moment, and attended by Mesdames de Flex and de Noailles. She was soon followed by her Royal brother and the bride, and the meeting between these long-severed relatives was stately and dignified. Anne of Austria, indeed, in whom the sister for a moment overcame the Sovereign, endeavoured to salute the Spanish King upon the cheek; but he held back his head so rigidly that she could not succeed.

The young Queen then threw herself upon her knees before her, and requested permission to kiss her hand; upon which Anne of Austria lifted her affectionately from the floor, and embraced her with great tender-ness. The conversation that ensued was kind, heart-felt, and earnest on the part of the Queen-mother; but Philip never relaxed for a moment in his stateli-ness. After some time had elapsed, the Cardinal Mazarin approached their Majesties, and informed them that a stranger was at the door, who requested that it might be opened to him; when Anne of Austria, with the consent of the King her brother, desired that the visitor might be admitted.

Mazarin and Don Louis had left the door partially thrown back, in order that the King might see his bride; and as it was desirable that she should also see him, they were careful not to impede her view, which was the more easy as he was a head taller than either of the Ministers. As her son approached, the colour of the Queen-mother rose, and the Infanta having met his eye, blushed deeply; while Philip remarked, with a gracious smile, that he had a handsome son-in-law.

The suite of the Spanish King consisted of Don Louis de Haro, his Prime Minister; Don Pedro of Arragon, Captain of the Bourgignon Guard; the Marquis d'Aytonne; the Marquis de Malepique, Grand Master of the Ceremonies; the Marshal of Leche and the Count of Monserci, both sons of Don Louis de Haro; Don Fernando Vonès-de Canto-Carrero, Secretary of State; and Senhors Pimentel and Velasquez. Louis XIV. was accompanied by the Queen-mother, *Monsieur* Duke of Orleans, the Prince de Conti, Cardinal Mazarin, and numerous great officers of the crown and kingdom; among whom were the Vicomte de Turenne, who had recently been appointed Marshal-General of the camps and armies of the King; and the Marshal Duke of Grammont, who had visited Madrid to demand the hand of the Infanta.*

The Infanta-Queen was attired in a robe of white satin, embroidered with bugles, and wore a hoop. Her hair was simply dressed, and adorned with a bouquet of pear-shaped emeralds mingled with brilliants, which were a present from her Royal bridegroom. On casting his eyes over the suite of Louis, the King of Spain remarked M. de Turenne, and repeated several times,

* Le Comte Alexandre de Laborde.

"There is a man who has caused me many uneasy hours:" a reminiscence which considerably annoyed the Marshal.*

When Louis XIV. had advanced to the centre of the saloon, the two Kings placed themselves in front of their respective tables, and cushions were brought to each; after which the Cardinal came forward, bearing a copy of the Gospel with a cross resting upon the volume, while the patriarch of India acted similarly on the Spanish side; both being in full costume. This done, the two Sovereigns knelt; M. de Brienne, French Secretary of State, then took the treaty of peace, and Don Fernando Vonès-de Canto-Carrero, who held the same distinguished rank in Spain, did the same; and each read it aloud in his own language. At its conclusion, the Royal allies laid their hands upon the Gospel, and took their oaths to observe its contents; after which they both rose, and advancing at an equal pace to the division of the apartment, exchanged an embrace, which Louis XIV. gracefully followed up by the assurance that he pledged himself, not only to peace, but to friendship. When some further courtesies had been reciprocated, they moved side by side to the upper end of the table, where Don Fernando Vonès presented the Spanish retinue to the King of France, and the Cardinal made the French suite known to the King of Spain. At the close of this ceremony each Monarch retired to his closet to sign the treaty, and reappeared in the great saloon, where Philip IV. remarked to the Queen-mother, that as it was growing late, he would return to the island-palace on the fol-

* Mémoires de Mademoiselle de Montpensier.

lowing day at three o'clock. After this announcement the two Courts separated.*

On the morrow the Queen-mother returned alone to the island, desiring MADEMOISELLE and the ladies of her household to await her in her apartments, in order to receive the young Queen, who was to reside with her for a couple of days; after which the marriage was celebrated in the church of St. Jean-de-Luz. A raised platform extended from the residence of Anne of Austria to the entrance of the church, which was richly carpeted. The young Queen was robed in a royal mantle of violet-coloured velvet, powdered with fleurs-de-lis, over a white dress, and wore a crown upon her head. Her train was carried by Mesdemoiselles d' Alençon and de Valois,† and the Princess of Carignan. After the ceremony the Queen complained of fatigue, and retired for a few hours to her chamber, where she dined alone. In the evening she received the Court, dressed in the French style; and gold and silver tokens, commemorative of the Royal marriage, were profusely showered from the windows of her apartment.

All her Spanish retinue, including the Countess of Pleigo, her camarara-mayor, then took their leave, and departed for Spain, with the exception of five individuals: her confessor, her physician, her surgeon, her first waiting-woman, Malina, who had served the Queen her mother in the same capacity, and the nephew of the latter, who had married one of her femmes-de-chambre.

---

* Mémoires de Mademoiselle de Montpensier.
† The younger daughters of Gaston.

On the 15th of June the Court left St. Jean-de-Luz for Paris; and at Toulouse the Duke of Grammont, after the successful termination of his mission to Madrid, received the compliments of the Royal circle, and presented to the King the Marquis de Péguilain,* his nephew, a young officer who had distinguished himself in the last campaign. His personal advantages, his cheerful disposition, his brilliant conversation, and, above all, his tact in dispensing those frank and apparently unpremeditated flatteries which are so welcome to sovereigns, so won upon the young King, that Louis at once determined to attach him to his person by all the attractions of Court favour.

At Amboise the Royal party were met by the Prince de Condé, who came to present his son, the Duke of Enghien. At Chambord the Duke of Longueville paid his respects in his turn; and lastly, at Fontainebleau, the Duke of Lorraine and the Duke of Guise awaited the arrival of the King and Queen to pay their homage. Thence the illustrious *cortège* reached Vincennes, where they remained until the preparations were completed for their solemn entrance into the Capital, which ultimately took place on the 26th of August.

On the occasion of his marriage the King had hastened to recall from banishment both the Count of Vivonne and the Marquis de Mancini; and poor Mary, in her exile at Brouage, wept with joy to hear that her dearly-beloved brother had been chosen for the honour of bearing the train of MADEMOISELLE, even although it was the nuptials of the only man whom she had

* Afterwards Duke of Lauzun.

ever loved; for she saw in this distinction an earnest
of his future favour.

For herself she had no longer anything to hope;
the past was as a brilliant dream from which the present was a mere troubled waking. She looked around
upon the dreary state by which she was environed,
and tried to condense her secret thoughts, and to fix
them on the familiar objects amid which she tried to
believe that she was destined to wear away her life.
Until within a week of the Royal marriage she had
occasionally received letters from Louis; and if they
were not what they had once been, still she struggled
to close her eyes against the fact; but, since the Infanta had become Queen of France, no communication
had reached her. This was as it should be, she argued
to her own heart—the passion which had formerly
been her glory could now only be her shame. It
was right that he should forget her, as he had
done. But when the bruised heart spoke in its turn,
she buried her burning face in her spread hands, and
thought what a boon it would be to die.

Mademoiselle de Mancini dwelt only on the broad
outline of her misfortune—she did not waste a thought
upon its details; and even had she heard of the new
courtier whom the pleasure-loving Louis had attached
to his train at Toulouse, she would not have suspected
for an instant that he could possess the power further
to embitter her destiny. And yet so it was: since the
banishment of Vivonne and Mancini, the young King
had only the faithful Prince de Marsillac about his
person to whom he was willing to confide those secrets
which at his age are considered as so important; and

even this confidence availed him little, for the Prince could only listen and lament. He did not possess sufficient courage to offer an opinion which might chance to give offence; and thus Louis soon wearied of a sympathy which, however sincere, was never suggestive.

At such a moment, therefore, M. de Péguilain was doubly welcome; towards the two recently reconciled culprits the King was anxious not to exhibit a too marked attachment, lest by so doing he might create jealousy and disaffection among his other courtiers; while as regarded the new favourite he was under no such restriction; and as De Péguilain was too clever not to perceive in an instant the error of the Prince de Marsillac, he at once adopted a diametrically opposite line of conduct, whose very novelty increased the predilection of Louis in his favour. He even dared to blame where he disapproved; but he did it with a grace which invested the error with a sort of kingly virtue that flattered the vanity and self-appreciation of the young Monarch, even although it convinced him of his fault; while, where he had only to applaud, he based his praises upon such high and dignified grounds that they assumed a double value.

It was not long, therefore, under these circumstances, ere Louis confided to him all the details of his passion for Mary de Mancini; a passion which, although chilled and diminished by recent circumstances, was still far from being wholly overcome; and the subtile Péguilain, desirous to remove so dangerous a rival from the mind and affections of his Royal master, employed his most crafty arguments to uproot the

lingering remains of so formidable a preference. He
urged nothing on the ground of morality, for he felt
that such a position was untenable in the atmosphere
of a Court; but he adduced his own example, and that
of some of the most gallant nobles of the kingdom, to
prove that constancy was a chimera fit only to be
entertained by boys and prudes. Day after day these
conversations were renewed; and if they failed to convince his auditor, they at least served to shake his
faith both in his own sentiments and in the merits of
Mademoiselle de Mancini; and hence the utter silence
on his part which supervened.

Such was the position of the former lovers, when
Madame de Venelle received an order from the Cardinal to conduct his nieces to Paris; asserting that
the Queen-mother, who had graciously expressed
her regret that Mary had not been present at the
Royal marriage, was anxious that she should at
least partake of the festivities which were consequent
upon them, as well as the entry of the young Queen
into the Capital. To Mademoiselle de Mancini this
order was like a death-pang; but she well knew that
there was no possibility of resistance, and she accordingly set forth upon her journey with a heart full of
despair and bitterness. As she advanced towards the
Capital, deaf to the joyous acclamations of her young
sisters, to whom a return to the pleasures of the Court
was as the opening of a new paradise, she saw at the
entrance of every town and hamlet the preparations
which were making to welcome the young Queen:
the triumphal arches, the windows garlanded with
flowers, and the many-coloured lamps forming the

cipher of the new deity; while, more than once, the
crowd recognising the livery of Mazarin, had stopped
the carriage to ask tidings of the progress of the
Royal party.

The heart of Mary bled at every pore, and when at
length she alighted at the new palace of the Cardinal,*
she hastened to shut herself into her apartment, in
order to indulge her despair in solitude and silence.

Mazarin, anticipating some outbreak on the part of
the unhappy girl, upon an occasion of such bitter trial,
resolved to seize the opportunity of offering to her at
that moment a brilliant marriage, which would place
her beyond the comments of the Court; and a letter
was accordingly put into her hands, immediately after
her arrival in Paris, in which he informed her that the
constable, Prince Colonna, had asked her hand, and
implored her to reflect seriously before she renounced
the prospect of becoming one of the greatest ladies in
Rome.

But Mazarin did not understand his niece. The
moment which he had considered to be so favourable
was precisely one in which Mary, who felt that her
dignity had been compromised by others, was more
than ever resolved to uphold it in her own person.
She consequently lost no time in returning a cold and
positive refusal to the proposition, and thus proved
that she was equal to the emergency, cruel as it
might be.

The communication of the Cardinal was followed by
a second from the Duchess of Noailles, in which she
announced the arrival of the Court at Fontainebleau,

* Now the Royal Library.

where the principal persons of the kingdom were to be presented to the young Queen previously to her entry into Paris; and in this list the names of Mary and her sisters having been inscribed, the Duchess wrote to inform her that they would have the honour of being presented by the Countess of Soissons, their sister, and the Princess of Conti, their cousin, on the ensuing Sunday, immediately after the high mass.

When Mademoiselle de Mancini reached Fontaine-bleau, every one was struck by the alteration in her person; they had one and all forgotten to estimate the extent of her sufferings; and, as though everything conspired to render her trial the more difficult to bear, just as she had begun to congratulate herself on hearing that the King had walked into the park to inspect the recent improvements of Le Notre,* and had with tolerable firmness joined her sister, and advanced towards the Queen, Louis entered the hall of audience to request Maria Theresa to accompany him in a second survey.

It chanced that at that precise moment the Countess of Soissons was in the act of presenting Mademoiselle de Mancini; and, as she was named, the King bowed without one vestige of emotion or sign of recognition; inquired after the health of the Cardinal, who had been detained at Vincennes by the gout; exchanged a few words with Madame de Soissons; and then turned away to salute the other ladies who were passing be-

---

* Andrew Le Notre, born at Paris in 1613, became architect and landscape-gardener to the King. He designed the grounds of Marly, Trianon, Chantilly, St. Cloud, the Tuileries, and the Terrace of St. Germain. In 1675 Louis XIV. conferred upon him letters of nobility, and the cross of St. Lazarus. He died in 1700.

fore the Queen, to each of whom he addressed some remark or compliment with the same condescending indifference.

Mary felt that she could bear no more. The whole brilliant scene swam before her eyes, but she could not distinguish objects ; and, suddenly rousing herself from an emotion which she felt would expose her to the merciless railleries of the circle, she withdrew a little apart in order to rally her scattered senses. The affectionate greeting of the Queen-mother added a fresh pang to her wretchedness; for it was so marked that she at once felt the security which it implied. She was no longer feared. Louis had then, indeed, ceased to love her.

When the presentations had terminated, the King invited all the ladies of the circle to attend the Queen at a hunt in which she was about to join ; and as every one rose, Mademoiselle de Mancini, eager to escape the scene of her torture, announced to the Princess of Conti that she had just received news of the aggravated illness of the Cardinal, which compelled her immediately to depart for Vincennes.

At some distance from the chateau she was compelled to halt, in order to allow the Queen and her train to pass ; and thus she again saw Louis, who preceded the cavalcade on horseback, surrounded by all the nobles of his Court, and conversing with the Marquis de Péguilain. The heart of Mary throbbed almost to bursting; it was impossible that the King should not recognise the livery of her uncle—the carriage in which he had so often been seated by her side —he would not—he could not pass her by without one word. She deceived herself. His Majesty was laughing at some merry tale of his new favourite, by which he was so much engrossed that he rode on, without bestowing even a look upon the gilded coach and its heart-broken occupant.

On the morrow, pale, cold, and tearless, Mademoiselle de Mancini drove to Vincennes, where she announced to the Cardinal that she was ready to give her hand to the Prince Colonna, provided the marriage took place immediately, and that he wrote without an hour's delay to ask the consent of the King. Mazarin, delighted to have thus carried his point after having despaired of success, at once promised to comply with her wishes; and Mary returned to Paris as self-sustained as she had left it, although, perhaps, not without a latent hope that her resolution would awaken some return of affection in the breast of Louis—induce some remonstrance—elicit some token of remembrance.

Again, however, she was the victim of her own hope. The Royal consent was granted without a single comment, accompanied by valuable presents which she dared not decline; and Mary walked to the altar as she would have walked to the scaffold, carrying with her an annual dower of a hundred thousand livres, and perjuring herself by vows which she could not fulfil.

Her after-career we dare not trace. Suffice it that the ardent and enthusiastic spirit which would, had she been fated to happiness, have made her memory a triumph for her sex, embittered by falsehood, wrong, and treachery, involved her in errors over which both charity and propriety oblige us to draw a veil; and if all Europe rang with the enormity of her excesses, much of their origin may surely be traced to those who, after wringing her heart, trampled it in the dust beneath their feet.

CHAPTER III

SHORTLY after the presentation at Fontainebleau,
the King and Queen entered Paris in state ; and
throughout the entire day the streets presented only
one long, and brilliant, and unbroken procession. At
four o'clock in the morning, every one was astir ; and
at five, all the ladies were in full costume, wearing
their mantles of ceremony, which they had no opportunity of throwing off until seven o'clock in the evening, notwithstanding the intense heat. The whole
Court was grouped about a throne which had been
erected at the barrier, and on which the young Queen

received the salutations of the several bodies of the state, before making her entry into the city. Neither the form nor colour of the houses before which the procession was to pass could be distinguished, so profusely were they decorated with hangings of tapestry and bright-tinted cloths; while the ground was thickly overstrewn with flowers and sweet-scented herbs, upon which the carriages moved without noise, extracting, as their heavy wheels crushed out the juices of the perfumed carpet beneath them, a thousand delicate odours. The Queen, in all the glory of her youth and beauty, glittering with jewels and beaming with smiles, was borne forward in an antique car blazing with gold, beside which rode her Royal Consort, attired in a suit of velvet embroidered with gems, estimated at between seven and eight millions.

The Queen-mother, accompanied by the Queen of England and the Princess Henrietta, occupied the house of Madame de Beauvais, within the city, where they awaited the termination of the preparatory ceremonies. The most magnificent feature of the whole procession was, however, the household of the Cardinal, which was numerous and splendid, totally eclipsing, by its marvellous pomp, that of *Monsieur;* in short, so regal in its profusion, that the Count of Estrées,* not

* John d'Estrées, born in Picardy in 1624, originally embraced the military profession, and was appointed Lieutenant-General in 1655. Created Vice-Admiral of France, Duke and Peer, he was commissioned to demand from the English an explanation of the spoliations which they were committing in the French possessions in America. In 1672, his vessels, in conjunction with those of England, overcame the naval forces of the Dutch Admirals, Ruyter and Tromp. On his return from this expedition he was made Marshal of France, and despatched in pursuit of the corsairs of Tunis and Tripoli. Ultimately he received the command of the coasts of Brittany, and died in 1707.

being altogether able to excuse its overwhelming assumption, could find no other terms in which to
describe it, than by styling it a display of *ostentatious
simplicity*.

This period must be considered as the culminating
point of Mazarin's prosperity. The people by whom
he had been driven from the Capital, and who had put
a price upon his head, received him with acclamations; the magistrates who had fulminated the decree
hastened to offer him their homage; the King acqui-
esced in all his wishes with the docility of a pupil,
conscious that he owed much of his present power to
his able and zealous policy. He refused to give his
hand to the Princes of the Blood in the third degree,
as he had formerly done; and he who had been
treated by Don Louis de Haro as an equal assumed to
consider the Great Condé as an inferior. Like his
predecessor, the Cardinal de Richelieu, he maintained
the same military household as the King himself, and
was surrounded by guards, gendarmes, and light-horse,
with, moreover, the addition of a company of musket-
cers, which bore his name, all commanded by nobles,
having young men of quality serving under them.*
He was no longer accessible as he had once been; and
any one who was ill-advised enough to ask a favour of
the King personally was certain of failure; while the
Queen-mother, by whom he had so long been upheld,
through good and evil fortune, against the whole sense
of the kingdom, became a mere cipher from the moment in which he ceased to require her protection.

One check, however, the haughty Cardinal was

* Mémoires du Duc de St. Simon.

destined to receive, even in the hour of his triumph; and that one came from the long-persecuted Stuart. Charles II. had solicited the hand of Mary de Mancini when he was a wandering exile, and it had been abruptly, and even superciliously denied. Mazarin had no sympathy with unthroned and wandering monarchs, but when the united voices of a great nation summoned Charles to take possession of his birthright, the spirit of the ambitious Cardinal yearned to clutch the recovered crown, and to place it upon the head of one of his nieces. He accordingly made known his change of resolution to the English King, offering him, at the same time, a dower of five millions of livres if he would raise Mary to the throne of England; but Charles spurned at the indelicacy of the proposal; and Mazarin forthwith encouraged the pretensions of the Roman Prince, to whom he ultimately married his unhappy niece.

The position of Mazarin necessarily secured suitors to the remainder of those young girls, of whom, on their first appearance at Court, the Marshal of Villeroy had uttered so brilliant a prophecy; and among these were the Dukes of Lorraine and Savoy, who, alike careless of receiving a dower with their brides, asked only that one fortified town on the borders of each principality should be placed under his own authority. This proposition Mazarin, however, absolutely rejected, considering such a concession dangerous to the interests of France, and the Princes accordingly withdrew their claim.

While the negotiations were proceeding at the Isle of Pheasants, a marriage had, however, taken place

which excited great indignation at the French Court.
The Princess Marguerite of Savoy, smarting under the
indignity which had been cast upon her at Lyons, and
foreseeing that an alliance was inevitable between
Louis XIV. and the Infanta, had, somewhat abruptly,
bestowed her hand upon the Prince of Parma—an
event which filled all the courtiers of France with astonishment.   They could not comprehend how a
Princess who had ever entertained a hope of sharing
the throne of Louis XIV. could abase herself to marry
a mere sovereign Prince.   They considered this step
as an immense dereliction from dignity, corresponding
but little with the haughty self-respect she had evinced
upon the rupture of her marriage with the French
King, and which had been a theme of general praise;
and they at once decided that, after having been encouraged to raise her eyes to such a height as that of
the French throne, she should never have condescended
to marry elsewhere, and would have been better advised had she retired into a convent.   They forgot
that she possessed all the pride of a woman as well as
the dignity of a Princess, and that nothing remained
to her save to prove that although she might have
writhed under an insult it had failed to crush her.

In Paris, meanwhile, all was gayety and splendour;
and the whole winter was consumed in one round of
never-ceasing dissipation, of which the two Queens
were, however, the least interested partakers.   Anne
of Austria was gradually becoming more and more
devout, and consequently less able to appreciate the
pleasures of the world; while Maria Theresa, naturally
timid, was ill at ease in the midst of a numerous and

brilliant Court. The natural consequence ensued: another circle more consonant to the tastes and habits of the fastidious courtiers was soon formed; and the most distinguished members of the nobility, both male and female, revenged themselves upon the monotonous and rigid ceremony of the Royal festivals by constantly frequenting the saloons of the Countess of Soissons, who, as superintendent of the Queen's household (to which exalted post she had been appointed by the Cardinal at the period of the Infanta's marriage), had apartments in the Tuileries, where, by her profuse expenditure, her wit, and, above all, her unconquerable audacity, she soon succeeded in making her circle the centre of gallantry, plotting, and intrigue.

The principal feature of her receptions was the perfect freedom which they permitted, all the guests being more or less connected, and all strangers resolutely excluded; and there Louis XIV., feeling, like his courtiers, the charm of an utter freedom from restraint, which he could never enjoy in his own apartments, spent evening after evening, unconsciously acquiring that grace and ease of manner by which he was so eminently distinguished in after-life.* His vanity and his ambition had been alike flattered by an alliance with the crown of Spain, and these, superadded to the youthful beauty of his wife, had deceived him for a time into the belief that he returned an affection which on her part was at once ardent and sincere; but he soon awakened from the happy illusion, and discovered that the void in his heart, left by the absence of Mary de Mancini, was by no means supplied.

* Mémoires du Duc de St. Simon.

In the midst of these courtly diversions, the Cardinal, hourly sinking as he was in health, determined to invite the King and Queen to a grand ballet, which should transcend all that had yet been seen at Paris; and he accordingly caused the Gallery of Kings to be decorated with columns of gold serge on a ground of red and green, which had been manufactured at Milan; but, in the course of hanging these costly draperies, they by some means took fire; and the magnificent roof of the gallery, painted by Fremine, and representing Henry IV. under the figure of Jupiter exterminating the Titans, was utterly destroyed, as well as all the Royal portraits executed by Janet and Porbus.†

This shock overcame the Cardinal, who considered it as an evil omen; and made no effort to escape, until he was aroused from his stupor by the Captain of his Guard, who supported him with some difficulty from the room, pale, trembling, and terrified to such an excess, that those who saw him under the influence of this morbid horror at once felt that its result must be fatal. The apartment in which he had been sitting was in flames an instant after he had been removed. He was conveyed to the Mazarin palace, where his physician was instantly summoned, and had no sooner ascertained the state of his patient than he called in eleven of his professional brethren; and when the consultation had terminated, at once returned to the sick-chamber, and announced to the Cardinal that although science might enable them to prolong his existence for

† Peter Porbus was a native of Ghent, who established himself at Bruges, where he acquired considerable reputation. The portrait of St. Hubert, at Ghent, and that of the Duke of Alençon, at Antwerp, are esteemed as his best works. He died in 1583.

a certain period, his malady was beyond cure, and must, ere very long, terminate fatally.

Mazarin received this intelligence with more firmness than could have been anticipated, and merely requested to be informed with equal frankness of the probable duration of his life. On being told that he might still survive a couple of months, he replied that two months would suffice for all that he had yet to accomplish; and bade the physician leave him, and during his absence consider how he could best further his fortunes; after which he retired to his closet to meditate upon the great change that awaited him.

Some days afterwards he sent to request that *Monsieur* would pay him a visit, and during the interview presented him with fifty thousand crowns; and thenceforward every one was convinced that he felt his end to be rapidly approaching.

His weakness increased hour by hour, while the declaration of Guénaud that he had only two months more to live was continually present to him by day and haunted his dreams by night. On one occasion, when Brienne * entered his chamber on tiptoe, the valet-de-chambre of his Eminence having warned him that his master was dozing in an armchair beside the fire, the visitor discovered that he was convulsed with agitation, although evidently in a profound sleep. His body rocked to and fro, impelled by its own weight; and his head swung from the back of his chair to his

---

* Henry Augustus, Count of Brienne, who died in 1666, leaving behind him his Memoirs, commencing at the accession of Louis XIV., and terminating at the death of Mazarin. Originally secretary to the Cardinal, he afterwards became an Ambassador, and Minister for Foreign Affairs.

knees, as he flung himself to the right and left inces-
santly; and during the lapse of five minutes that M.
de Brienne continued to watch his movements, he
asserts that the pendulum of a clock did not vibrate
more rapidly than the frame of the sufferer. At intervals he uttered a few words, but in so low and
choked a voice that they were unintelligible; and at
length Brienne, unable longer to endure so wretched a
spectacle, and fearful lest the sick man should fall into
the fire, summoned his attendant from the antechamber
to his assistance.

As he was aroused from his troubled sleep, the
Cardinal betrayed the secret which was preying upon
his vitals; the name of his physician and the period of
existence which had been assigned to him were the
first sounds that escaped his livid lips; and when those
about him endeavoured to cheer him by the remark
that Guénaud was only mortal, and his judgment consequently fallible, he answered, with a heavy sigh, that
Guénaud understood his trade!

Yet still, despite this moral and physical prostration,
the indomitable Minister turned his attention to the
establishment of his remaining nieces, and affianced
Hortensia, the most beautiful of the two, to the Duke
of la Meilleraye, Grand-Master of the King's household,
on condition that he should assume the name of Mazarin, with an annual income of fifteen hundred thousand
livres, and immense personal effects. To Marianne,
who was yet a child, he moreover bequeathed a sufficient dower to enable her to enter the family of
Bouillon when her age should permit her to do so;
while, as regarded the Princess of Conti and the

Countess of Soissons, he had already secured to the former the superintendence of the household of the Queen-mother, and to the latter that of the reigning Queen. Hortensia, to whom, despite the affection which he had long felt for her, he had always denied everything beyond common necessaries, herself relates the delight which she experienced when, so soon as her marriage had been determined on, her uncle called her into his cabinet; and, in addition to a splendid *trousseau*, presented to her a casket containing ten thousand pistoles in gold. The Cardinal had no sooner left her at liberty to examine her new acquisitions than she sent for her brother, the Marquis de Mancini, and her sister Marianne, and desired them to take what they pleased. All the trio then filled their pockets; and as, when they had done this, there still remained about three hundred louis in the casket, they opened the windows, and threw them into the court of the palace, in order that the lacqueys who were assembled there might scramble for the prize.

This adventure soon reached the ears of the Cardinal, and the ingratitude and folly which it exhibited added another pang to his dying hours, which had already become embittered by a sudden remorse on the subject of his enormous wealth. The Cardinal de Richelieu, a man of high birth and ancient family, had felt that he had a right to possess a princely revenue; but Mazarin, whose origin was at best equivocal, and who had been the architect of his own fortunes, at whose extent he learned to shudder in the solitude of a death-chamber, became terrified as he reflected that he was able to bequeath more than forty millions to his family.

His confessor, a conscientious Théatine monk,* startled like himself at the unheard-of amount of his wealth, which Mazarin mentioned in the course of his confession, allowing that he considered it as a sin; at once declared that his Eminence would be damned if he did not forthwith make restitution of that portion of the money which had been ill acquired; to which the Cardinal rejoined that he owed all to the bounty of the King. The honest ecclesiastic was not to be deceived, however, by such a compromise with principle, and retorted, with the same firmness, that the Cardinal must compel himself to distinguish between what he had actually received from the Sovereign as a free gift and what he had himself appropriated; upon which Mazarin, in despair of such an announcement, declared that in that case he must restore the whole. He then reflected for an instant, and desired that M. Colbert might be immediately sent to his apartment.

When Colbert had obeyed the summons, the Cardinal confided to him the difficulty which had arisen;

---

* The Théatines were a religious order, instituted in 1524 by St. Gaétan de Thienne, Peter Caraffa, Bishop of Théato, afterwards Pope under the name of Paul IV., and several other distinguished persons. Clement VII. sanctioned the institution, in 1529, under the name of regular clerks: a novel description of priests, living in a community, and forming different societies or congregations, some of which exacted solemn vows, others merely simple ones, and others again from whom no vow whatever was required. The Théatines were the first community who bore the appellation. The name of Théatines was given to them in consequence of the Bishop of Théato having been one of their founders. They wore a black frock, a black cloke, and white stockings. They undertook to reform the clergy, to instruct the young, to nurse the sick, and to contend against heretics. Throughout all France they possessed only one establishment, which was situated in Paris. Their order was suppressed and their convent destroyed in 1790. The Théatines produced many individuals who distinguished themselves both by their science and their virtues.

and the former at once advised, in order to remove his scruples, and to prevent his immense fortune from passing away from his family, that he should make a donation of all that he possessed to the King, who would not fail in his royal generosity to annul the act at once. Mazarin approved the expedient; and on the 3d of March the necessary document was prepared; but three days having elapsed without the restoration of his property, he became the victim of a thousand fears; and as he sat in his chair he wrung his hands with agony. The wealth for which he had toiled and sinned—which he had wrenched alike from the voluptuous noble and the industrious artisan, had, as he believed, passed away from him forever. The labour of his life was rendered of none avail; and the curses which he had accumulated upon his own head had failed even to gild his tomb. "My poor family!" he exclaimed at intervals; "my poor family! They will be left without bread."

This bitter suspense was not, however, fated to be of long duration. On the third day from the transmission of the deed of gift, Colbert entered his chamber radiant with success, and placed the recovered document in his hands, with the intelligence that the King had defini- tively refused to accept the offering; and that he authorised the Minister to dispose of all his property as he should see fit. On receiving this assurance, the worthy Théatine declared himself satisfied, and at once bestowed the absolution which he had previously withheld; and he had no sooner done so than Mazarin drew from beneath his bolster a will which he had already prepared, and delivered it to Colbert.

A week before his death a singular whim seized the
sick man: he caused himself to be shaved, his mous-
taches to be trimmed, and covered his cheeks with red
and white paint, to a degree which rendered his complexion more fresh and brilliant than it had ever been
during his period of health.   He then entered his chair,
and made a tour of the gardens despite the cold Feb-
ruary wind, to the great astonishment of the courtiers
who were dispersed in the avenues; but the effort was
beyond his strength, and he soon fell back upon his
pillows, desiring that he might be conveyed to his
apartment.*

Meanwhile the King continued to pursue his usual
amusements, dancing in the different ballets, and sup-
ping with the Queen-mother; but the illness of the
Minister at length became so grave that all business
was suspended.   The marriage of Hortensia had taken
place, but necessarily without any of those festivities
by which it would, under other circumstances, have
been attended; and her husband had at once assumed
the name of Duke of Mazarin.

From the time that the Cardinal received the last
sacraments, the courtiers were excluded from his
chamber; and ingress was forbidden to all save the
King, the Queen, and M. de Colbert.   During one of
his visits, Louis entreated that the Minister would give
him whatever advice he might deem desirable, declaring his intention to profit by it to the utmost.

" Sire," said the dying man, " know how to respect
yourself, and you will be respected: never have a
Prime Minister; and employ M. de Colbert whenever

* Louis XIV. et son Siècle.

you require the assistance of an adviser at once intelligent and devoted."

It was on this occasion also that he made use of nearly the same words in which, as we have mentioned elsewhere, he was himself presented by the Cardinal Bentivoglio to the Cardinal Barberino: "I owe everything to you, Sire; but I believe that I cancel my obligation to your Majesty by giving you Colbert."

Ultimately the Cardinal expired early in the morning of the 9th of March, "more like a philosopher than a Christian," * at the age of fifty-two, having ruled the kingdom of France during a period of eighteen years. He was scarcely regretted even by those whose fortunes he had founded; neither the King nor the Queen-mother made any show of grief beyond the first few days; and so little was either really affected by the decease of the man who had, whatever might be the other vices of his administration, raised France to a high and dignified station among the nations of Europe, that Louis, on awakening in the morning, no sooner ascertained his death than he immediately rose, and summoned Letellier, Fouquet, and Lionne to a secret council, in which he informed them of his future intentions; after which he had an interview with the Queen-mother, with whom he dined, and subsequently left Vincennes, where the Court was then residing, in a close carriage, for Paris; while Anne of Austria, twice widowed in fact, although not in heart, followed in a chair with bearers, attended by the Marquis de Beaufort, her first equerry, and Nogent-Bautru, her jester, who enlivened her journey by their unceasing gayety.

* Louis XIV., sa Cour, et le Régent.

The administration of the kingdom was regulated two days before the death of the Cardinal according to his advice, and every arrangement had been already made when Harlai de Chanvalon, the President of the ecclesiastical assembly, waited upon the King to inquire to whom he must in future address himself on questions of public business, and received the concise reply, " *To Myself.*"

St. Simon asserts that it was, doubtless, the enormous wealth accumulated by the Cardinal which decided Louis XIV. to dispense, throughout the remainder of his reign, with a Prime Minister, as well as to exclude all ecclesiastics from his council. Well, indeed, might he form such a resolution; for the fortune which Mazarin left behind him was colossal, and his will declared the disposal of fifty millions, while, at the same time, it strictly forbade an inventory of his personal effects.

His principal legatee was Armand Charles de Laporte, Marquis de la Meilleraye, Duke of Rethelois de Mazarin, to whom he bequeathed all that might remain of his property after the acquittal of the several legacies, and who never ascertained the exact amount of his inheritance in consequence of the interdict which the Cardinal had laid upon the inventory, although he succeeded in convincing himself that it ranged between thirty-five and forty millions. The Princess of Conti, the Princess of Modena, the Princess of Vendôme, the Countess of Soissons, and the Princess Colonna, each received two hundred thousand crowns. The Marshal of Mancini, who had anticipated the entire inheritance of his uncle, and who was, consequently, dissatisfied with his bequest, had, for his portion, the Duchy of Nevers, nine hundred thousand crowns in ready money, a yearly income derived from his estate of Brouage, the moiety of his personal effects, and all his property in Rome.   To the Marshal of Grammont he left a hundred thousand livres, and to Madame de Martinozzi, his sister, an annual income of eighteen thousand.

The special legacies were these :   To the King, two cabinets filled with public records, in an unfinished state; to the Queen-mother, a brilliant, estimated at a million of livres ; to the reigning Queen, a bouquet of diamonds ; to *Monsieur*, sixty gold marks, a hanging of tapestry, and thirty emeralds; to Don Louis de Haro, the Spanish Minister, a fine painting by Titian ; to the Count of Feusaldagne, a large clock in a gold case ; to his Holiness the Pope, six hundred thousand livres, to be employed in the war against the Turks ; to the poor, six thousand francs ; and finally, to the crown, eighteen large diamonds, to be called the Mazarins.*

Upon a survey of the enormous wealth thus amassed by one man, during an administration of twenty years, for a great portion of which period the nation had been drained of its resources both by foreign and intestine war, it is scarcely surprising that the Cardinal should have been anxious to conceal, as far as possible, the exact amount of which he had pillaged the people.

In 1630 he had barely emerged from obscurity, and had, for all fortune, his diplomatic subtilty and his indomitable ambition; while, in 1661, he died possessed

* Louis XIV. et son Siècle.

of a sum equal to two hundred millions of the money
of the present day. He died unmourned even by his
own family, every member of which he had raised to
rank and opulence; for his avarice had counteracted
the effect of his exertions. Each felt that he was
striving rather to exalt himself through them than to
benefit their individual fortunes; while they resented
the parsimony which, after decorating them with a
rank requiring a corresponding expenditure, left them
in a position that prevented their upholding it with
dignity. The results of such a system might have
been foreseen; the Princess of Conti and the Duchess
of Mercœur, from the fact of their having married
shortly after their arrival in France, escaped its effects;
but M. de Mancini and his remaining nieces became,
so soon as they acquired the means, improvident and
careless to a degree exceeding belief.

In short, the avarice of Mazarin had passed into a
proverb, and both friends and enemies were subjected
to its withering effects. Every circumstance afforded
him a pretext for augmenting his hoards; and his favourite axiom, whenever he was thwarted, of " They
sing, they shall pay for it," was never once contradicted
throughout his whole period of power. He is, moreover, accused, by more than one authority, of having
stooped to measures degrading to his high rank, in order to increase his property, and is even suspected of
having shared with the privateers the profits of their
ocean forays, although this fact was never fully proved;
but the Dutch did not hesitate to brand him with a
moral degradation which they would never have assigned to the Cardinal de Richelieu.

Mazarin felt no compunction in cheating at cards, which were, at that period, the ruling passion of the Court, and, miser as he was, habitually risked the gain or loss of fifty thousand livres in a night; while, as a natural consequence, his temper ebbed and flowed with his fortune.

Perhaps the most amusing anecdote connected with his avarice, multitudinous as they were, was an equivoque which occurred only a few days before he breathed his last, and within an hour after he had obtained the absolution which his confessor had, for a time, withheld. The Cardinal had just transmitted his will to Colbert when some one scratched at the door,* which having been interdicted, Bernouin, his confidential valet-de-chambre, dismissed the visitor.

"Who was there?" asked Mazarin, as his attendant returned to the bedside.

"It was M. de Tubeuf, the President of the Chamber of Accounts," replied Bernouin; "and I told him that your Eminence could not be seen."

"Alas!" exclaimed the dying man, "what have you done? he owed me money; perhaps he came to pay it; call him back—call him back instantly."

M. de Tubeuf was overtaken in the anteroom and introduced. Nor had the Cardinal deceived himself. He was, indeed, come to liquidate a heavy gambling debt, and Mazarin welcomed him with as bright a smile as though he had years of life before him in which to profit by his good fortune, took the hundred pistoles

* At this period bells were unknown in France, and every courtier carried, in the pocket of his vest, a small comb with steel teeth, with which he scratched against the door of the apartment where he desired to enter.

which he had brought in his hand, and asked for his jewel-casket, which was placed upon the bed, when he deposited the coins in one of the compartments, and then began to examine with great interest the valuable gems which it contained.

"You must give me leave, M. de Tubeuf," he said, with emphasis, as he lifted a fine brilliant and passed it rapidly across the light, "to offer to Madame de Tubeuf ——"

The President of Accounts, believing that the Cardinal, in acknowledgment of the heavy sums which he had from time to time gained at the card-table, on his account, since he had been too ill to act for himself, was about to present him with the precious gem which he then held in his trembling fingers, moved a pace or two nearer to the bed with a smile upon his lips.

"To offer to Madame de Tubeuf"—repeated the dying miser, still gazing upon the jewel—"to offer to Madame de Tubeuf—my very best compliments." And, as he ceased speaking, he closed the casket, and made a sign that it should be removed.

Nothing remained for the discomfited courtier but to make his bow and depart, with the mortification of feeling that he had been, for an instant, so far the dupe of his own wishes, as to believe, that while he was yet alive, Jules de Mazarin could make up his mind to give away anything for which he had no prospect of receiving an equivalent.*

* Louis XIV. et son Siècle.

CHAPTER IV

IN order to dissimulate as much as possible the general joy which was felt by all classes on the demise of the Cardinal, the King resolved upon a general mourning. The order was unprecedented, for it compelled not only the Court, but all the Princes of the Blood to assume a mourning garb for a Minister who was himself neither a Prince, nor related, in the most remote degree, to the Royal family. There was, however, no alternative; for the King and the two Queens having given the example, nothing remained but to follow it; and the Court was, accordingly, crowded with sable garments and smiling faces, producing an anomaly as striking as it was inconsistent.

The death of Mazarin filled the Court with the wildest hopes and the most active intrigue. The pretty women who figured in the Royal circle flattered themselves that a Prince of two-and-twenty, who had once been sufficiently the slave of his passions to offer his crown to a subject, might be easily governed under the influence of a new attachment; the younger of the courtiers indulged the belief that the reign of favour-itism was about to recommence, while each of the Ministers anticipated individual supremacy. Not one among all those who were the most intimately inter-ested in the progress of events suspected for a moment that Louis XIV., the deity of the Court ballets, the slave of etiquette, and the unquestioning and supine pupil of an ambitious Minister, would suddenly rouse himself from his moral lethargy, and take upon him the burden of the government.

Nothing could more distinctly prove the error under which all the great functionaries laboured with regard to their young Monarch than the fact that not one of them demanded a personal audience of his Majesty, but that each inquired to whom he was in future to address himself. We have already stated that his an-swer was " *To* MYSELF ; " but even startled as they were by such a reply, they never anticipated that he would persevere in a resolution so dissonant to his habits. They had been accustomed to consider him only as the votary of pleasure, and they had yet to learn that for some time past he had tried his strength, and re-solved to fill worthily the exalted station which Providence had assigned to him as a birthright. Determined to become in fact, as well as in name, the Sovereign of France, and remembering that, both by precept and example, Mazarin had warned him never again to subject himself to the despotism of a Prime Minister, he stringently defined the limits beyond which no public functionary might presume to act, and indicated to each the particular hour at which he was to report his proceedings to himself, giving to all the necessary power which alone could render their Ministry effective, but watching over each with a tenacity of attention that rendered any abuse of authority impossible, or at least dangerous.

We have already stated that, immediately on ascertaining the demise of Mazarin, Louis XIV. had summoned to his presence Le Tellier, Lionne, and Fouquet; and they are personages too important to be passed over without a formal introduction to the reader.

Michel le Tellier, the War Minister, was a man of handsome exterior and winning manners, timid in domestic life, but courageous and enterprising in politics—tolerably firm in pursuing measures once adopted, but, nevertheless, better calculated to follow than to lead. His greatest dread was that of becoming unpopular; and he was, perhaps, encouraged in this somewhat weak alarm by the consciousness that he was himself a dangerous enemy. He was mild and insinuating, always profuse in promises, which he was equally ready to forget, and eminently courteous and accessible; but his regard did not extend beyond these professions. His utter want of ambition was exhib-

ited in a piece of advice which he offered to the King
on the subject of the Chancellor Seguier, who was
anxious to be elevated to the rank of a Duke and
peer: "Such exalted dignity, sire," he replied, when
consulted by Louis XIV., "does not beseem the
learned professions, it is good policy to accord them
only to military prowess:" a decision which blighted
all the exertions and hopes of his eldest son (Louvois),
who never succeeded, despite his eminent services, in
effacing from the mind of his Royal master the remark
made by his father, who had assuredly never reflected
on the probable consequences of such an opinion in
his own family. Louvois was the victim of this unguarded aphorism; but Seguier was eventually exempted from its influence, for he ultimately obtained
the coveted rank which was denied to the able son of
the Minister.*

Hughes de Lionne was a gentleman of Dauphiny,
and a more able diplomatist than his colleague, Le

---

* Michel le Tellier was the son of a Councillor of the *Cour des Aide*
(exchequer), and was born in Paris in the year 1603. He was, in the
first place, a Councillor of the Grand Council, then (in 1631) King's
Advocate at the Chatelet of Paris, and Master of Requests. Appointed Steward of Piedmont in 1640, he secured the favour of Mazarin, who made him War Secretary of State, and to whose interests
he remained attached throughout the whole of the civil war. He was
intrusted with all the negotiations between the Court and the rebel
Princes, especially Gaston d' Orleans and the Prince de Condé; and
it was by his influence that the treaty of Ruel was ultimately concluded.
After having been the Minister of Anne of Austria during her Regency,
he continued to serve Louis XIV. in the same capacity. He co-
operated with Colbert in the overthrow of the Superintendent Fouquet, and obtained for his son, the Marquis de Louvois, the survivor-
ship of his office as Secretary of State. In 1677 he was made Chancellor and Keeper of the Seals, and in this trust he exhibited a zeal
both vigilant and active. He was one of the principal movers of the
revocation of the edict of Nantes. He died in 1685.

Tellier, a fact which was so well known to all the foreign Ministers that they redoubled their caution when
compelled to treat with him personally. Whenever a
necessity for exertion arose De Lionne was indefatigable, and fulfilled his arduous duties with a zeal and an
ability almost unequalled; but the crisis once passed,
he again turned all his energies towards those sensual
pleasures to which he was a willing slave, and sacrificed
without hesitation his fortune, his health, and even his
natural indolence, to the gaming-table, the banquet,
and other still more questionable vices.*

Nicholas Fouquet, whose name became famous,
owing to his extraordinary reverse of fortune, was a
man whose genius was essentially diplomatic. Full of
resources, of which he never hesitated to avail himself
to the utmost, he frequently discovered a means of successful enterprise in the very circumstances which to
others appeared pregnant only with danger, and hopeless from their entanglement. Learned in the law,
well read in polite literature, and an amateur of art—
brilliant in conversation, high-bred in his deportment,
and magnificent in all his ideas, he no sooner conferred
a service than he at once placed the person whom he
had obliged in the position of a friend, and confided in
his reciprocal esteem without one misgiving that it
would fail. He possessed, preeminently, moreover,
the rare and difficult talent of listening, not only with
patience, but with apparent interest, to the most dull
and vapid communications, and always replying at the
right moment and in the most agreeable manner, by
which means he generally contrived to dismiss those

* Mémoires pour servir à l'Histoire de Louis XIV. *Choisy.*

to whom he had given audience more than half satisfied, though they had not succeeded in inducing him
to admit their claims. A finished voluptuary, he never
suffered the duties of his ministry to interfere with the
pleasures to which he was addicted; but effecting to
retire to his villa at St. Mandé, in order that he might
work without interruption, he was accustomed to leave
a crowd of courtiers in his antechamber, loud in their
admiration of the indefatigable labour to which so great
a man devoted himself without comment or reluctance,
and to descend by a secret stair to a small garden,
where he abandoned himself to a most degrading dissipation, in the society of some of the most beautiful
and high-born women of Paris, who, seduced by his
gold, and careless of their own honour, became the
shameful partners of his disgraceful orgies.

Liberal to an excess towards literary men, whom he
was able to appreciate and anxious to reward, he became the friend of Racine, La Fontaine, and Molière,
the Mæcenas of Le Brun * and Le Nôtre; and he
pleased himself with the belief that he should be enabled to govern the young King by directing at the
same time his official labours and his private pleasures.
He deceived himself, however; for, as we have already
shown, Louis XIV. had resolved henceforward to act
by and of himself.

Such were the three individuals to whom, two hours

---

* Charles le Brun, an historical painter, and one of the heads of
the French School of Art, was born in Paris in 1619. He was laden
with honours and generosity by Louis XIV. His most famous works
are the *Battles of Alexander*, the *Penitent Magdalen*, the *Martyrdom
of St. Stephen*, etc. He also executed a great number of frescoes in
the chateau of Fouquet. He died in 1690.

after the death of Mazarin, the King announced his intention to become his own Prime Minister; and while Le Tellier and Lionne merely bowed somewhat incredulously, a smile played upon the lip of Fouquet. He held the key of the public chest; and accustomed as he was to guide all around him with a golden rein, he never doubted that in his case, at least, the Royal purpose must soon be rescinded.* Hitherto, whenever Louis had applied to him for a supply, he had contented himself by replying, " Sire, the treasury of your Majesty is empty ; but his Eminence will, no doubt, advance you a loan." Now, however, no further appeal could be made to the equivocal liberality of the Cardinal, and Fouquet felt that he was himself all-powerful upon the question of finance, while the profuse expenditure and uncalculating magnificence of the pomp-loving young Sovereign left him little doubt that his assistance would soon become imperative.

Accident, that providence of Princes, had, however, ordained otherwise. After a brief conference with his Ministers, Louis had forthwith proceeded to the Louvre; when, on entering his cabinet, the first person whom he encountered was Colbert, who had been awaiting him for the last two hours, and who requested a private audience upon the instant. Startled by the urgency of his manner, the King at once retired with him into the deep recess of the window, beyond the hearing of the courtiers, where Colbert informed him that he came to indicate to his Majesty the different places in which Mazarin had concealed or buried nearly fifteen millions of ready money, of which no mention

* Louis XIV. et son Siècle.

had been made in his will, and which he (Colbert)
consequently imagined had been intended by the Cardinal to replenish the treasury of his Majesty, which
was at that time utterly exhausted.   The young Sovereign listened with astonishment, and demanded to
know if he were certain of the extraordinary fact that
he advanced; to which Colbert replied by furnishing
him with proofs of his assertion.

No circumstance could have occurred at that particular moment so welcome to Louis XIV. as the discovery of this hidden treasure, which at once, and for
a long period, rendered him independent of the superintendent of finance; nor was the revelation less important to the fortunes of Colbert himself.

Immediate measures were concerted for the recovery
of the various sums designated by the zealous and
fortunate young secretary, and with almost universal
success.   At Sedan five millions were found, two at
Brissac, six at La Fère, and between five and six at
Vincennes.   A considerable sum had also been se-
creted in the Louvre; but although the spot where it
had been deposited was found, the money had disappeared; and it was then remembered that Bernouin,
the confidential attendant of the Cardinal, had left the
place on the previous evening for more than two hours
before the death of his master, and it at once became
apparent how the interval had been employed.

Despite this subtraction, however, Louis XIV. at
once found himself one of the richest monarchs of
Christendom; for his private funds amounted to no
less than from eighteen to twenty millions, of which
the value was greatly enhanced by the fact that no

one, not even Fouquet himself, was aware of the extent of his resources.

His first and most anxious care was to regulate the
etiquette of his Court, which had been necessarily invaded during the extreme and sudden changes to
which his reign had hitherto been subjected; for even
at this early period Louis XIV. began to manifest that
respect for his own individuality which he was not long
in exacting from all by whom he was surrounded.
He was then in his twenty-third year; and although
the Cardinal had, as a matter of personal policy, caused
his education to be so neglected as to expose him to
the frequent mortification of feeling his incapacity to
enforce opinions of whose validity he was himself convinced, but which he could not put forth with the
propriety exacted from him by a sense of his own
dignity, he was, nevertheless, in society, the model of
an accomplished gentleman. Of middling height, but
admirably proportioned, he increased his stature by
the adoption of high-heeled shoes, which raised him
some inches. His hair was magnificent, and he wore
it in masses upon his shoulders, after the fashion of
earlier times; his nose was large and well formed, his
mouth agreeable in its expression, his eyes of a deep
blue, and his mode of utterance slow and strongly ac-
centuated, lending to all he said a gravity incompatible
with his years, but which produced an effect admirably in accordance with the impression that he studied
to produce.

No contrast could be greater than that which existed
between the Royal brothers, both physically and mor-
ally. Philip of France was a Prince of gentle, or,

rather, of effeminate manners; of ardent, but merely
impulsive courage, and a perfect type of the luxurious
and chivalric nobility by whom the last of the Valois
had been surrounded, and who had served to distinguish his reign alike by their vices and their daring;
while, with these qualities, it will be readily understood
that Philip had long supported, with undisguised disgust, the superiority assumed by a brother who sought
to crush, by his overweening arrogance, all those who
were subservient to him. The whole boyhood of the
two Princes had consequently been one perpetual
struggle; but for the last few years the younger had
ceased to contend beneath the iron hand which had
ascertained the extent of its own strength.

Before the death of the Cardinal, *Monsieur* had
solicited the Queen-mother to obtain the consent of
the King to his marriage with the Princess Henrietta
of England; and Anne of Austria, who was tenderly
attached to the young Princess, readily undertook the
mission. Its accomplishment, however, proved to be
a matter of more serious difficulty than she had anticipated; for Louis had never overcome his boyish
prejudice against the daughter of Charles I., and excused himself by alleging that an alliance with the
English would be displeasing to the French people;
nor was Mazarin less repugnant to the marriage; for
he had still to resent the refusal of Charles II. to receive the hand of his niece, forgetting that the Monarch
was never likely, on his side, to forget that his alliance
had been coldly declined when he was in misfortune.
Nevertheless, the arguments of the Queen at length
prevailed over the distaste of her son; and it was

agreed between Anne of Austria and Henrietta-Maria, that the marriage of their children should take place immediately after the return of the latter from England. whither she was about to proceed with her daughter, in order to enjoy the happiness of seeing Charles II. at length peaceably in possession of the throne of his ancestors.

A short time subsequently to the arrangement, she accordingly took leave of the Court, to the great mortification of *Monsieur*, who was vehement in his entreaties that she would shorten her visit for his sake; and on arriving in London she found the Duke of Buckingham, the son of him to whom Anne of Austria was indebted for the most romantic episode of her life, enamoured of her widowed daughter, the Princess-Royal; but as, like his father, he professed but little constancy in his attachments, he had no sooner been presented to the Princess Henrietta than he became madly in love with this new divinity.

To the young and amiable Princess, the transition from an existence of constraint, monotony, and privation, to the glitter and gallantry of a Court like that of Charles II., was perfect enchantment; and she began for the first time to experience a happy consciousness of her own individual importance, which was enhanced by the constant receipt of letters from *Monsieur* to the Queen, urging her early return to Paris, and the accomplishment of her promise.

The Prince was, indeed, most anxious to terminate the marriage, not from any overweening attachment to his promised bride, for he was incapable of violent passion, but because he regarded it as an event which, by creating for him an independent position, must in some degree emancipate him from the authority of his brother; while Henrietta-Maria was the more inclined to comply with his entreaties from the desire which she felt to conduce to the comfort and consolation of Anne of Austria, who, after having seen herself all-powerful during the Regency, had lived to witness the gradual decline of her influence, and to feel herself a mere cipher in the brilliant Court which had once bowed down before her.

At the death of Mazarin she had made an effort to recover her lost authority; but Louis XIV. had no sooner detected the latent intention than he gave her to understand, what he had already declared to his Ministers, that he would brook no rival near his throne; and, moreover, that this was no sudden resolution, fated to be rescinded as lightly as it had been made, but a firm determination, long formed, and which would admit of neither expostulation nor argument.

The Queen-mother bowed beneath this last disappointment with a patient dignity which astonished all those who were conversant with the inherent haughtiness and impetuosity of her character, and began to prepare at her favourite Val-de-Grâce a retreat, in which the culture of flowers became her principal amusement. Few were yet aware that the fearful malady, to which she ultimately fell a victim, was already making fearful inroads on her constitution, and exposing her to concealed but terrible suffering. Under these circumstances, therefore, the English Queen decided upon leaving London without further delay, despite the inclemency of the season; and the Duke of Buckingham, at his earnest entreaty, received permission from Charles II. to escort herself and the Princess Henrietta to Paris.

During the voyage, the vessel in which they were embarked struck upon the sands, and was for a time in imminent danger of going to pieces; and it was during that awful interval that the Duke, utterly careless of himself, but maddened by the idea of the peril to which the Princess Henrietta was exposed, put so little constraint upon his passion that it soon ceased to be a secret to those about him. At length the vessel was, with considerable difficulty, rescued from its perilous position, but so much damaged that it was found necessary to put in to the nearest port, where it had no sooner arrived than the Princess was attacked by measles. At this new calamity the Duke became outrageous in his despair, and committed such excesses that the Royal party had no sooner anchored at Havre, where they were to remain a few days in order that the invalid might recruit her strength, than the Queen insisted that Buckingham should immediately set out for Paris to announce their arrival. Resistance was of course impossible, and on the evening of the same day the Duke proceeded on his mission.

Within a week he was followed by the Royal travellers, who were met by *Monsieur* at a considerable distance from the Capital, with all the eagerness of a lover—although, as we have seen, his demonstrations were in reality due to an influence less flattering to the Princess than that of her own charms. In his suite was the Count of Guiche, who had become his most intimate friend and favourite, and who was one of the most elegant nobles of the Court, and had, moreover, secured in the heart of Henrietta a feeling of gratitude for his gallant championship during the most cruel trial of her girlhood.

Buckingham's first folly in the Capital was to parade his jealousy of the Count of Guiche; and he did this with so little discretion that *Monsieur* was soon informed of the circumstance, and made a formal complaint to the two Queens, who affected to laugh at his uneasiness—the Queen of England, strong in the virtue of her daughter, and Anne of Austria in the belief that the power which she had possessed over the father would prove equally influential over the son.

Philip was, nevertheless, not to be appeased so easily: a rumour of the headlong passion with which the Princess Henrietta had inspired Buckingham had long been rife in Paris; and she who had, during so many years, been totally overlooked and utterly unappreciated, suddenly became the object of universal curiosity and interest. The jealousy of *Monsieur*, which was easily aroused, would have required no further stimulus than this one fact, even without the presence of the original culprit; but this annoyance, superadded to the other, was too much for his powers of endurance; and he consequently exacted that, after a brief sojourn at the French Court, sufficient to enable him to fulfil the necessary formalities of his mission, the Duke should be invited to return to England.

Meanwhile the preparations for the marriage were in active progress; and the King presented to his brother, as a wedding present, the appanage of the late Duke of Orleans, with the exception of Blois and Chambord; while the arrival of the English Princess, to the great delight of the Court, put an abrupt conclusion to the mourning for the Cardinal, which gave place to the fashions which she introduced.

From an interesting child, Henrietta, embellished by happiness, and by a consciousness of her exalted rank, had suddenly been transformed into a lovely and dignified woman. Tall and graceful, with a complexion of the most exquisite beauty, and possessed of a refined taste, which taught her to profit by her personal and acquired advantages, she saw herself at once the principal ornament of the most supercilious Court in Europe, and the model upon which all the great ladies of the Royal circle strove to fashion both their dress and their deportment. The revolution was a startling one; nor was the King himself exempted from its influence.

The austerities of Lent not permitting the celebration of any great public festivities, it was decided that the marriage of *Monsieur* should take place privately at the Palais-Royal, in the presence only of the Royal family, and the persons of their immediate retinue. On the 31st of March it was, consequently, performed by the Bishop of Valence, having for its principal witnesses the King and Queen, the Queen-mother, the Queen of England, the daughters of the late Duke of Orleans, the Prince de Condé, and the Duke of Buckingham; and a few days subsequently the latter left the Court of France in a state of mind bordering upon distraction.

At this period the King commenced the system of

regularity upon which he had already decided, and which became ere long the undeviating etiquette of the Court. He rose at eight o'clock, performed his devotions, dressed himself, and then read for an hour, at the close of which time he partook of a light breakfast; left his chamber at ten, attended the Council, and at midday heard mass; during the interval which remained until the dinner hour, he appeared in public, or went to the apartments of the two Queens; and after the repast he generally remained a considerable time with the Royal family. He then closeted himself with his Ministers, either collectively or separately; gave audiences, during which he exhibited great urbanity and patience; and received petitions, to which he replied on days previously reserved for that purpose. The rest of the afternoon he passed in conversation with the Queen and the Queen-mother, or in the little court of the Countess of Soissons; at the card-table, but never for a heavy stake, or at a mere game of chance; in driving, or at the theatre, according to the season; and this routine was never interrupted save during the hunting-season, or on the occasion of some extraordinary festivity. Finally, at supper, which was his favourite repast, he collected about him all the Princesses and their ladies of honour, and terminated the evening by ballets or assemblies.

At the end of April, the Court removed to Fontainebleau, where they were followed by the Prince de Condé and the Duke of Beaufort, who had become two of the most assiduous and popular members of the Royal circle; and a month had been spent in per-

petual fêtes, when the harmony which had hitherto
subsisted between all the members of the illustrious
family was suddenly interrupted by the awakened
jealousy of the young Queen, who one day threw herself at the feet of Anne of Austria, bathed in tears and
trembling with emotion, and confided to her, in the
anguish of her heart, that the King had fallen in love
with *Madame.*

The Queen-mother was more grieved than surprised
by this communication; for *Monsieur,* jealous on his
side, had already complained of the same fact; and
Anne of Austria had found herself unable, from internal conviction, to advance arguments sufficiently
powerful to remove the impression from his mind.

There was, indeed, too much reason for the uneasiness of both parties; for the King, who, during her
infancy, had not only felt, but unhesitatingly expressed, his contempt for the English Princess—and
who, when for a moment her marriage with himself
had been mooted by the Cardinal, had declared that
she was too thin, that she did not please him, and that
it was impossible for him ever to love her—had discovered, from the moment in which she became the
wife of his brother, that all their tastes and feelings
assimilated, and had attached himself to her society
with a tenacity that excited universal remark.

Nor was the Princess, on her side, altogether blameless. The depreciating remarks of the King had been
repeated to her during her girlhood, and had not only
produced a dangerous influence over her mind, but
become, unconsciously to herself, the motive of her
actions. Had any one ventured to tell her that, in

accepting the hand of *Monsieur*, when she might have commanded that of one of the reigning Sovereigns of Europe, she was impelled by the hope of forcing Louis to recant his opinions and to confess the power of the attractions which he had previously affected to despise, she would have been indignant at the accusation, while such was, nevertheless, the impulse under which she acted.

For this unacknowledged purpose—unacknowledged, doubtlessly even to her own heart—she had studied to become a proficient in all the graces which adorn a Court; in all the endearing qualities which are the best charm of woman, whatever may be her worldly rank; and in those intellectual qualities which could elevate her character, and render her superior to the mere butterflies by whom she was surrounded; and she had succeeded only too well in her attempt. Such combined attractions, both of person and mind, could not fail in their effect upon so susceptible a nature as that of Louis XIV.; and an intimacy ensued which, although perfectly warranted by the closeness of their family connection, was not without considerable danger to both parties.

There was a bitter exultation mingled with the triumph of the Princess, which can be appreciated only by those who, like herself, have been subjected to intense humiliation, and at last experience the power of revenging it upon its author. Henrietta did not believe for an instant that she could love the King; but she nevertheless rejoiced in the conviction that she could sway at will the feelings of the haughty Sovereign before whose insults she had formerly quailed; and she consequently left no effort untried to render her circle the centre of pleasure and attraction: the favourite amusements of Louis were those of most frequent recurrence in her apartments; the friends whom she selected were precisely those the best calculated to interest and occupy him. In short, ever bearing in remembrance that he had once ventured to underrate her merits and to reject her hand, she experienced a cruel satisfaction in perceiving that she had established her power over the heart of the King.*

As Louis held his Court sometimes in her apartments, and sometimes in those of the Countess of Soissons, a close friendship was soon formed between them; but the young Queen resolutely refused to become a sharer in their amusements. Sincerely attached to Anne of Austria, whom she rarely quitted; rigid in her devotional duties, and more retiring in her habits than was consistent with her rank, she could ill brook the partial desertion to which the difference in their habits condemned her; and she began to suspect a truth which was well calculated to embitter her existence.

Despite the beauty of Maria Theresa, upon which Louis XIV. had congratulated himself at their first interview, he had never for an instant loved her. His heart was yet unweaned from a first and serious attachment, and no stranger could replace its object. He treated her, indeed, with the greatest consideration, both as a Princess of Spain and as the Queen of France; but so cold a feeling could not satisfy a young and enthusiastic nature. Moreover, Maria Theresa was unfortunate enough to love her husband with all

* Mémoires de Madame de Motteville.

the ardour of her country; and she found herself estranged from his society, and compelled to seek her
only amusement in speaking the language, and in
dwelling upon the memories of her lost home with the
Queen-mother. As a sense of her moral isolation
grew upon her, she shrunk more and more resolutely
from the overpowering gayeties of the Court, and
sought to escape the harrowing spectacle of the gallantries bestowed by Louis upon the bevy of beauties
by whom he was estranged from her society—thus
unconsciously widening the gulf between them, and
rendering the very estrangement over which she wept
in secret the more habitual and hopeless.

And while the young Queen thus mourned with
bitter tears the loss of an illusion which had rendered
the period of her marriage one proud and triumphant
dream, each day appeared to strengthen the attachment
between the fickle Monarch and his brother's wife, although no word of passion had polluted the lips of
either. Neither the remonstrances of the Queen-
mother, the prospect of the early birth of a Dauphin,
nor the arduous labours of the state to which he had
condemned himself, diverted the attention of Louis
XIV. from his devotion to *Madame;* and the magnificent fêtes which he instituted in her honour were a
source of such enormous outlay that Fouquet was lost
in astonishment as to whence the Sovereign could derive the means of sustaining so profuse and uncalculating an expenditure, and awaited with some anxiety
the exhaustion of his resources, in order that he might
at last attain the coveted ascendency over his mind
through the medium of his necessities.

It was probably with a view to remove the too legitimate suspicions of the Queen, by diverting them into another channel, that Louis, about this time, affected a violent inclination for Mademoiselle de la Motte Houdancourt, one of her maids of honour. These ladies were under the guardianship of the Duchess of Navailles,* who owed her place at Court to the Cardinal. Some privileges, contested between herself and the superintendent, excited the indignation of Madame de Soissons, who, in common with her sisters, had shown the greatest indifference on the death of the Cardinal; but who, nevertheless, taunted the Duchess by the remark, that in opposing the niece she was guilty of ingratitude towards the uncle; to which Madame de Navailles replied with calm dignity, that, could his Eminence return to earth, he would be more satisfied of her gratitude than of that of the Countess of Soissons.†

The position of the high-principled and scrupulous Duchess of Navailles was already sufficiently arduous before she raised up so powerful an enemy as the heartless and vindictive Countess, who never forgave the stinging rejoinder which we have just quoted; for a spirit of gallantry had become diffused over the

---

* Wife of Philip de Montault, Duke of Navailles, and de la Valette, peer and Marshal of France; originally of Bigorre, where his family traced their descent from the 14th century. Born in 1621, he entered the household of the Cardinal de Richelieu as a page in 1635, abjured the Protestant religion, and attained to the highest military grades. He commanded the right wing of the cavalry at the battle of Senef, in 1674; and, in the following year, received the bâton of Marshal of France. He afterwards obtained the ribbon of the Order of the Holy Ghost, and the post of Governor of the Duke of Orleans. He died in 1684, without male issue.

† Souvenirs de Madame de Caylus.

Royal antechamber, which rendered her office by no
means a sinecure.   Nevertheless, Madame de Navailles
continued to struggle against, not only the intrigues
of the young nobles who enjoyed her perplexity, but
also the folly of the giddy maids of honour themselves, who were but too willing to second their enterprise; for she felt that the dignity of her Royal
mistress was compromised by the levity of her charge,
and she resolved at any sacrifice to enforce regularity
and order.

Madame de Soissons had consequently a double
motive for encouraging the coquetries of Mademoiselle
Houdancourt; as, by so doing, she screened *Madame*
on the one hand, and exasperated the Duchess of
Navailles on the other; and the pupil whom she had
selected proved so apt, that, ere long, Madame de
Navailles had reason to apprehend that Louis contemplated an invasion of her apartments.   The rumour
had no sooner reached her, therefore, than she hastened
to request a private audience of the King, with whom
she expostulated both as a Christian and as a husband,
about to bring disgrace beneath the roof of a young
and virtuous wife; and for a time he supported her
harangue with so much urbanity, that she began to
hope she had convinced him of his error.   She was,
however, premature in her judgment.   The imperious
nature of Louis XIV., which loathed even the semblance
of opposition, and his extreme selfishness, which led
him to disregard every consideration that clashed with
his own self-indulgence, soon prompted him to hint to
the zealous Duchess that she was incurring a great
risk of exciting his displeasure; to which she respect-

fully, but unhesitatingly replied, that she had already reflected upon the probability that such would be the case, and was aware of all the misfortunes which the loss of his Royal favour must inevitably entail upon her; being conscious that it was to his Majesty both her husband and herself owed alike their fortune and their position—he the lieutenancy of the light-horse, and she her situation as lady of honour, of both which his Majesty could in a moment deprive them; but that this fact, urgent as it was, could not alter her resolution to fulfil her duties conscientiously; and then, throwing herself at his feet, she implored him to respect the household of the Queen, and to remember that he was himself its master.

The King dismissed her angrily; but, on the morrow, chancing to find her in the circle of the Queen-mother, he advanced and greeted her with a smile and an extended hand; and Madame de Navailles flattered herself that peace had thus tacitly been signed between them.* If, however, Louis were really sincere at the moment, this better feeling did not long endure; for, having detailed the scene to Madame de Soissons, she sarcastically congratulated him upon his patience; and the vanity of the King at once led him to pursue an adventure from which his better sense would have dissuaded him: and by thus making himself the tool of an ambitious woman, who was only anxious to mortify a rival, he subjected himself to a mortification unworthy of his exalted rank, and of the example which it enforced him to offer to the giddy courtiers about him.

* Mémoires de Madame de Motteville.

On the other hand, the conscientious lady of honour, feeling, as she had frankly confessed to the King, that the prosperity of her family depended upon his favour; and anxious not to ruin her husband, save on valid and sufficient grounds, consulted her confessor, explaining the difficulty in which she found herself, and her determination to abide by his decision. It was soon given; for he at once declared that, as a Christian, she was called upon to sacrifice all worldly advantages rather than fail in her duty by an unworthy concession. The alternative was, nevertheless, a bitter one; and it was not without a great struggle that Madame de Navailles saw herself compelled to disregard all worldly considerations, in order to prove herself worthy of the confidence which was reposed in her; and the rather, as her resistance against aggression involved not only herself but her husband, whose position was also one of trust and dignity; but she never wavered; and, finding her best consolation in the conviction that she could only suffer in a good cause, she remained firm in her resolution; and, being given to understand that she must place no faith in the apparent repentance of the King, she immediately caused iron gratings to be placed outside the windows of the apartments of the maids of honour.

This extreme step did not, however, entail all the consequences which she had apprehended; for Louis contented himself by dismissing her from her guardianship of the very troublesome office to which she had been appointed, and conferring it upon the superintendent, who would, as he had good reason to know, prove less unaccommodating. This result, which formed a subject of conversation for all the Court, sufficed to terminate a fancy which had never, upon the part of Louis, been a serious one; for even at the period when it commenced, his attention had already been attracted by Mademoiselle de la Vallière—that La Vallière, whose name was destined to become famous throughout Europe, and whose gentleness and devotion almost excused the errors which have thrown a veil of reproach over her name.

There never was, in all probability, an autobiography written, either by man or woman, which bore so thoroughly the stamp of truth and feeling as that of Mademoiselle de la Vallière; and there is no attempt, from the first page to the last, to palliate her fault, of which no one was a more severe critic than herself. Never for a moment deceived as to the extent of her error, it embittered even the most brilliant moments of her existence; and nothing, save the intense affection which she lavished upon the King—not as a Sovereign, but as a man—not as the Monarch of France, but as the one and only individual who ever touched her heart—could have induced her so long to disregard the reproaches of a conscience which neither pomp nor passion had ever power to silence for an hour.

CHAPTER V

LOUISE-FRANÇOISE DE LA BAUME DE
BLANC, the daughter of the Marquis de la
Vallière, was born at Tours in the year 1644. She lost
her father almost in her infancy; and her mother, who
was the daughter of the Seigneur de la Coutellaie,
equerry of the King's state stable, was left with a proud
name and an inadequate income, which induced her to
form a second marriage with M. de St. Rémy, who
held the situation of controller of the household of
Gaston, Duke of Orleans. At the Court of that
Prince, Louise passed the early years of her girlhood,
while her only brother, the Marquis de la Vallière,
whom she seldom saw, spent the principal portion of
his time at Tours. As she advanced to girlhood, the

to the monotonous little Court of *Madame*, who welcomed her with kindness, and where, without becoming officially one of her maids of honour, she was
invested with all the privileges of the office, and
passed most of her time. The circle of a Prince,
banished virtually, if not ostensibly, from the Capital,
offered no very great attractions to persons of her age;
but to Louise the companionship of other young girls
rendered the Palace of Blois a paradise; for she
guessed not how soon the serpent of passion was to
glide among the roses of her peaceful Eden.

We have already recorded the brief visit paid to
Blois by Louis XIV., when on his way to the frontier
to claim the hand of the Infanta: a visit apparently so
unimportant, and yet so fraught with consequence to
at least two individuals, that it could not be passed
over in silence. During the few hours of its continuance, Mademoiselle d'Orleans lost the last glimpse of
the hope to which she had so fondly clung of seeing
herself one day upon the throne of France; while
Louise de la Vallière learned that the idolised and
powerful Sovereign of whom she had always thought
with awe almost amounting to alarm, had, on his departure from Blois, awakened her to the existence of a
new world of feeling, in which she found herself alone,
hopeless, and bewildered. Now, for the first time, she
began to understand the conversations which were
daily taking place in the anteroom among her weary
and discontented companions, who were constantly
bewailing their exile from the Courtly festivities of
Paris. Now she began to comprehend that life might
indeed present objects of greater interest than her

birds, her flowers, or her sports; but the conviction
was confused: she never entertained an idea that she
loved the King; she merely pictured to herself the
happiness which must arise from seeing him, listening
to his voice, and existing in his presence; and her
own misery in being exiled, as she believed forever,
from such a privilege.

And meanwhile Louis was on his way to Fontarabia,
criticising the old-fashioned little Court of Blois, and
unconscious of the very existence of the fair and bash-
ful girl whose whole being was absorbed in the memory of his transitory visit.

The illness and subsequent death of *Monsieur* supervened; and while she wept over the loss of her protector, Louise de la Vallière little suspected the effect
which it would produce on her own fortunes.   The result to her family was, indeed, sufficiently serious to
absorb her attention, even at that early age; for, by
this event, M. de St. Rémy was deprived of his office,
and his pecuniary resources were painfully affected.
On the dispersion of the regal establishment, some
months subsequently, Louise, with an overburdened
heart, walked to the palace to take leave of Mademoiselle de Montalais, her favourite friend, who had
been appointed to a place in the household of the
Princess Henrietta, then betrothed to the King's
brother; and the departure of this lady was so bitter a
trial that she was faint with weeping when she arrived
at the chateau, and found herself in the presence of
Madame de Choisy.   Her grief was so evident and so
sincere that the wife of the Chancellor was touched by
her emotion, and inquired if she would like to share

flowers, or her **sports**; but ....
.... she never .... an ....
.... the King, she merely pictured to .... the
happiness which must arise from seeing him, ...
to his voice, and existing in his presence, ...
own misery in being exiled, as she believed forever,
from such a privilege.

And meanwhile Louis was ...... his way to Fontarabia,
criticising the old-fashioned little Court of Blois, and
unconscious of the very existence of the ...... and bash
ful girl whose whole being was absorbed in the mem
ory of his transitory visit.

The illness and subsequent death of .... super-
.... and while she wept over the .... her pro-
.... Louise de la Vallière little .... the effect
.... it would produce on her own fortunes. This re-
.... to her family was, indeed, sufficiently serious to
.... their attention, even at that early age; for, by
the .... M. de St. Rémy was deprived of his office,
and his pecuniary resources were painfully affected.
On the dispersion of the regal establishment, some
months subsequently, Louise, with an overburdened
heart, walked to the palace to take leave of Mademoiselle de Montalais, her favourite friend, who had
been appointed to a place in the household of the
Princess Henrietta, then betrothed to the King's
brother; and the departure of this lady was so
trial that she was faint with weeping when ......
at the chateau, and found herself in the .... of

.... Her grief was .... and
of the Chancellor was touched
quired if she would like to show

the fortunes of her old companion by entering the household of the Princess.

Louise smiled amid her tears. " In that case," said Madame de Choisy, " wipe your eyes ; for all the arrangements are not yet made, and there will be room for you."

The promise was fulfilled. At the termination of a fortnight the appointment arrived ; and a week was allowed to the young maid of honour for the necessary preparations. Within that week the marriage of *Madame* took place ; but Mademoiselle de la Vallière only entered upon her duties previous to the departure of the Court for Fontainebleau, where she was suddenly launched into a world of dissipation, splendour and intrigue. She was soon remarked by the Count of Guiche ; but although she received his attentions with gratitude, she repulsed his gallantries and avoided his society.

At this period she had just attained her seventeenth year ; and, even while eclipsed in beauty by many of those about her, the charm of her unaffected modesty, the retiring timidity of her manner, the extreme purity of her complexion, her large and languishing blue eyes, and the profusion of flaxen hair which shaded her brow and bosom, gave a singular loveliness to her appearance, of which she alone was unconscious. Her figure, which was not yet formed, and a slight lameness, occasioned by a fall during her girlhood, were the only defects which even her enemies could discern in her appearance, save, perhaps, a slight trace of small-pox, which had in some degree impaired the smooth-ness of her skin ; and, meanwhile, her peculiarly unobtrusive habits exempted her on all sides from either jealousy or suspicion.

Among the festivities at Fontainebleau a ballet took place, in which both the King and *Madame* bore an active part; Louis XIV. figured on the occasion as Ceres; and the *Grand Monarque*, who resented the most trifling want of respect from those around him, made his appearance in a Greek tunic and a coronet of golden wheat-ears; declaimed his own praises in the rhymes of Benserade; and, finally, figured in this un-regal costume before the eyes of the whole Court.* At the termination of the ballet, the company dispersed themselves about the park, where they found in every direction tables sumptuously provided, of which the honours were done by nymphs and forest deities, crowned with ivy; but all these magnificent arrangements were almost unheeded by Mademoiselle de la Vallière, who was absorbed by the image of the King-goddess, whom she had so lately seen exhibiting the graces of his person amid applauding crowds; and she at length felt the gayety by which she was surrounded so oppressive that she suggested to Mesdemoiselles de Chalais, de Tonnay-Charente,† and de Montalais, that they should walk into the forest and repose themselves for a time in one of its dim recesses.

To this proposal they willingly consented; and after strolling for awhile, listening to the nightingales and watching the stars, which from time to time peeped

---

* "The ballet of *The Seasons* was danced by his Majesty, at Fontainebleau, on the 23d of July."—*Gazette de* 1661.

† Afterwards Madame de Montespan.

through the foliage as it swayed beneath the voluptuous breeze of evening, they finally seated themselves under a large tree upon the border of the wood, and began to discuss anew the pleasures of the day and the chief actors in the gay scene which had formed their principal feature.   For a time Louise bore no share in the conversation; but she was at length startled from her silence by an appeal to her judgment, when she unguardedly declared that she could give no opinion upon the subject discussed, and was only surprised that any man should be remarked beside the King.

This reply drew down upon her, as a natural consequence, the sarcasm of the whole party, who accused her of being so difficult that nothing save a crowned head would satisfy her vanity; when the poor girl, anxious to exculpate herself from a charge which she felt must overwhelm her with ridicule, should it become the gossip of the Court, hastily exclaimed that they did her injustice; for that his crown could add nothing to his natural advantages; but was, on the contrary, the safeguard of those about him, as without it he would indeed be doubly dangerous.

She had no sooner made this unwise rejoinder than she became aware of the extent of her imprudence; and while her three companions remained silent in astonishment, she sprung from the ground to escape, and discovered that two men were partially concealed behind the tree against which she had been leaning.   A faint shriek instantly directed the attention of the whole party to the fact, and, terrified beyond control, they simultaneously fled in the direction of the chateau, where they arrived panting and breathless.

Once alone in her apartment, whither she immediately hastened, Louise de la Vallière wept bitterly
over the folly of which she had been guilty.   It was
the first time that she had ventured to express her feelings, and the long-pent-up secret had escaped her she
knew not how, although she was painfully conscious
of the ridicule with which it was calculated to overwhelm her.   In the agony of her repentance she flung
herself upon her knees, and earnestly prayed that the
consequences of her fault might be averted; but her
emotion and alarm were, nevertheless, so great, that
for a couple of days she was unable to perform her
duties, or even to leave her room.   Now, for the first
time, she felt in their full force the difficulties of the
position which she had coveted; and she trembled as
she looked forward to again appearing before the
malicious eyes of the Court.   There was, however, no
alternative; and she was at length compelled to make
the trial.

Montalais was, as she well knew, the greatest gossip-
monger in the whole city; while Mademoiselle de
Tonnay-Charente, who piqued herself upon her wit,
was not likely to suffer so favourable an opportunity
for its display to remain unimproved; and thus, beset
on all sides, and only too well aware of her own want
of self-possession, the poor girl stole from her chamber on the evening of the third day to take her place
in the saloon of *Madame*.   She traversed the anteroom without exciting either word or look which implied the betrayal of her secret; and for a moment she
began to entertain the hope that she had wronged her
companions, and that her folly was undivulged; but a

remark from the Duke of Roquelaure, who chanced to be in the circle of *Madame* when she entered, soon undeceived her; and the shock was so great that she staggered, and would have fallen, had not Mademoiselle de Tonnay-Charente promptly come to her assistance, attributing her sudden faintness to fatigue: a plea of which she readily availed herself to request her dismission for the evening.

When she found herself again alone, the unhappy girl more than ever saw the necessity of struggling against a weakness which could only tend to increase the difficulty of her position, and, at whatever cost, to combat the terror and shame by which she was oppressed. Having formed this resolution, she entered the apartments of *Madame*, on the following day, with an apparent composure which belied her real feelings.

As she had anticipated, the King was already there, and engaged in conversation with the different ladies of the suite, carefully addressing a few words to each as he passed down the room. He was yet at some distance from the door near which she sat, and thus she saw him slowly approach, and began to comprehend that she should probably be spoken to in her turn: an honour which had never yet occurred to her, and which caused her heart to beat with mingled joy and apprehension. At length, as she had anticipated, he paused before her, and inquired what she had thought of the ballet of the previous Saturday, if, indeed, she still remembered it?

With some difficulty she compelled herself to answer; but her agitation was increased by remarking

that the King started as he heard her voice, and looked
at her with a marked attention which drew upon them
the observation of all by whom they were immediately
surrounded. After remaining a few seconds with his
eyes steadily fixed upon her, Louis, with a profound
bow to the blushing and bewildered girl, prepared to
leave the room; but, before he did so, he again turned
more than once towards the spot where she was sitting.

Thenceforward Mademoiselle de la Vallière found
herself the marked object of the attentions of the
King; and, fortunately for her composure, she continued unaware that his Majesty had been one of the
eavesdroppers of the wood of Fontainebleau, induced
to this somewhat treacherous indiscretion by the sug-
gestion of M. de Beringhen, who, seeing the four fair
girls retire from the brilliant scene around them to hold
a conference in the forest, had laughingly remarked,
that they were about to confide to each other the
secrets of their hearts, and that the opportunity was a
favourable one for ascertaining the identity of their
favourite cavaliers. The King had entered willingly
into the jest; but as it was too dark to permit either
himself or his companion to discover who were the
fugitives, they were compelled to trust to their after-
penetration to divine this important point; and thus it
was that Louis XIV., jealous above all things of being
loved for his own sake, had the gratification of discovering that one heart at least acknowledged the power
of his attractions, not as a monarch, but as a man.
The sequel of the incident we have already shown;
and when he recognised the voice of Mademoiselle de
la Vallière, it was scarcely wonderful that he should

examine with attention the person of whose attachment he had obtained such unequivocal testimony.

The delight of Louise was consequently great, when
she perceived that the King looked upon her with an
eye of favour; while his manner was at the same time
so guarded, and so respectful, and he so carefully ab-
stained from any allusion which could lead her to look
beyond the present moment, or to imagine that his
courtesy was intended to imply more than a mere
generous interest, that she soon found herself enabled
to converse with him with easy and graceful composure; and thus to exhibit all the charm of a young,
pure heart, still uncontaminated by its commerce with
a Court.

Every evening, when he joined the circle of *Madame*,
after having paid his respects to the Princess and the
principal ladies of her circle, he contrived to secure a
brief conversation with Mademoiselle de la Vallière;
and as the passion of Louis for *Madame Henriette*
was at least suspected, it became a matter of general
belief that it was for her sake alone he made his visits
so long and so continuous: a faith which Louise entertained in common with those about her, and which
blinded her to the peril to which she was exposed.

One individual alone was not, however, to be so deceived, and that one was the Count of Guiche, who, as
we have already stated, had been attracted by the
modest graces of La Vallière from her first appearance
at Fontainebleau; and conscious that should this new
caprice of the King gain strength by time, he could no
longer entertain the hope of succeeding in his own
suite, he resolved at least to ascertain its effect upon the

mind of Louise herself; for which purpose he paid a visit to her apartments, where he exhibited a jealousy which terrified the poor girl into a remonstrance upon the unreasonableness of his reproaches, unmerited on her part, as she had never felt or affected towards him a warmer feeling than that of respectful esteem. Nevertheless the Count was not to be appeased; and conscious of the weakness of his cause, he overwhelmed her with the most stinging sarcasms, and finally withdrew, declaring that although she had despised his passion, he doubted not but it would prove acceptable elsewhere.

This outbreak of offended vanity in a man whom she had avoided was a sincere annoyance to Madamoiselle de la Vallière, who had the greatest reason to apprehend the effects of his enmity from the fact that he had latterly attached himself exclusively to *Madame*, while there could not exist a doubt but the same circumstance which had excited the annoyance of M. de Guiche must have awakened the indignation of the Princess, and that the sudden alliance which had been formed between them owed its existence to their mutual mortification. Be this as it may, however, it is certain that the intimacy thus commenced ultimately led to the unfortunate attachment which endured throughout their lives.

Only a few days subsequent to the visit of the Count of Guiche a great hunt took place, at which all the ladies of the Court were present; and at the termination of the sport, tables were spread under the trees in the park, at a considerable distance from the chateau, about which the whole party assembled. The repast was a gay one, but the heat excessive, while the clouds which were gathering above their heads foretold a storm. Nevertheless, heedless of the warning, the feast proceeded; nor did it suffer any interruption until the large drops that had been for some time plashing heavily upon the leaves, suddenly gave place to a burst of rain, which descended in such torrents that all idea of etiquette was forgotten; and the different individuals of the Royal party rushed away in every direction to shelter themselves as best they might.

In the confusion, Mademoiselle de la Vallière was running she knew not where, when she found the King beside her, who, politely taking her hand, hurried her towards a large tree, whose massy foliage offered a sure protection from the storm. Grateful for such distinguished care, but conscious of the observation it would not fail to create, Louise would have retired; but the first words of the King, full of grave reproach, arrested her purpose; and throughout the whole of the two long hours that the storm endured, remorselessly pouring down upon feathered toques and satin draperies, it was remarked by those who were sufficiently near to note the circumstance, that Louis remained bareheaded, with his plumed hat in his hand; and that he maintained an earnest and animated conversation with his fair companion, to which only one interpretation could be given.

Thenceforward the King avoided all particular notice of Mademoiselle de la Vallière, when they met in the apartments of *Madame;* but when, in the evening, the ladies drove through the different avenues of the park, he quitted after a time the carriage of the Prin-

cess, and mounting his horse, soon stationed himself
beside the window of that which was occupied by
Louise—while not content with thus expressing the
increase of his passion, he sustained with her a daily
correspondence, which convinced her only too well,
had such a conviction still been wanting, of the extent
of his attachment and the refinement of his mind.

Alarmed by the extreme beauty and eloquence of
the letters which she thus received, lest the compara-
tive imperfections of her own style should shock
the taste of her Royal admirer, Mademoiselle de la
Vallière at length decided, after painful misgivings and
an almost unconquerable reluctance, to apply to the
Marquis de Dangeau * to undertake the task of replying to them, little suspecting that those which had
so much excited her apprehension proceeded from the
same pen.   Nor, strange to say, would this fact ever
have transpired had not La Vallière herself, on an occasion when she felt oppressed by the compliments of
the King on her rare talent, confessed to him with a
trembling heart that she was unworthy of his praises,
and revealed the name of their true author.   To her
great relief, Louis was equally frank, and they were

---

* Philip de Courcillon, Marquis de Dangeau, was born in La
Beauce in 1638.   He commanded a troop of cavalry under Turenne,
and distinguished himself in Flanders in 1658.   After the peace of the
Pyrenees, he offered his services to Spain, which was then endeavouring to reconquer Portugal; and, on his return to France in 1667, he
served throughout the campaign of Lille, and attended the King in
all his expeditions as aide-de-camp.   In 1673-4, he was appointed
envoy-extraordinary to the electors of the Rhine, Governor of
Touraine, and Councillor of State.   His talents also caused him to
be elected a member of the French Academy, and the Academy of
Science.   Dangeau died in 1720, leaving behind him his *Memoirs*,
and a *Journal of the Court of Louis XIV.*, in 58 quarto vols. MS.

enabled to laugh together over their mutual misgivings. This little incident, however, trifling as it was in itself, exhibited, in their common friend, a discretion so rare at Court, that it founded the fortunes of M. de Dangeau.*

At that period the fashion of lotteries had obtained greatly at Court, and the Queen-mother, who, despite her increasing malady, was anxious not to be altogether overlooked, although unable to leave her own apartments, was one of the most constant in providing these entertainments, to which, having only a small circle of her own, she was careful to invite *Madame* and her immediate friends and retinue. On one occasion the King drew the principal prize, which was a pair of bracelets of great value, when an immediate anxiety was felt to ascertain to whom they would be offered, although little doubt was entertained that they would become the property of *Madame Henriette;* and, accordingly, all eyes were turned in her direction, to detect at once the mingled pleasure and triumph with which she must welcome such an offering.

Meanwhile, Mademoiselle de la Vallière stood apart, thinking not of the ornaments, but of the hand which held them, and anxious merely for the moment when, released from the trammels of her service, she should once more see the King at her side, and listen to his words addressed only to herself. For a moment Louis sat motionless with the glittering baubles in his hand, as his keen eye swept the circle, and then slowly rising, he made his way through the throng of ladies, and presented them to La Vallière, who, having attentively

* Louis XIV. et son Siècle.

examined their workmanship, returned them with a profound courtesy, remarking that they were indeed extremely beautiful.

"In that case, Mademoiselle," said the King, graciously, "they are in hands too fair to resign them;" and, with a salutation as stately as her own, he returned to his seat.

Madame bit her lip and turned pale; but she soon recovered her self-possession, and made her acknowledgments most gracefully for the honour conferred upon one of her own suite, while the Queen looked on with a quiet smile, utterly unsuspicious of the truth. Feelingly does La Vallière exclaim, as she records this incident of her life, "That confidence was a sad misfortune for us all. One tear from her would have saved me!" *

While the passion of Louis was augmenting from day to day, heightened by jealousy of every one who approached its object, a new candidate for the favour of the fair maid of honour presented himself in the person of the Superintendent of Finance, Nicholas Fouquet, who, accustomed to see everything yield before the power of his gold, never doubted for an instant that he should be as successful in his pursuit of Mademoiselle de la Vallière as he had proved with so many other ladies of the Court; and, accordingly, proceeded with little scruple and less delicacy to make his designs known to her, and to solicit her affections. He was, however, so coldly and sternly repulsed, that any other suitor would have comprehended at once that his pursuit was hopeless; but Fouquet was un-

* Mémoires de Madame de la Vallière.

accustomed to opposition, and disdained to perceive discouragement in the frowns of an indignant woman. Merely, therefore, changing his tactics, he deputed Madame du Plessis-Bellièvre, who was one of his fastest friends, to mention to his new idol that he had at her service the sum of twenty thousand pistoles, if she would condescend to accept it. Outraged by the proposal, La Vallière fixed her eyes steadily upon the unworthy messenger, and, in a voice audible to all the circle, she desired that M. Fouquet might be informed all further advances on his part were needless, as twenty millions would not induce her so to degrade herself.

It is believed that this circumstance, which soon reached the ears of the King, contributed, in no trifling degree, to hasten the fall of the depraved Minister; but Louis XIV. was by no means the only individual in his empire who had vowed the ruin of the licentious Superintendent. M. de Laigues, who had privately married Madame de Chevreuse, and who was dissatisfied with Fouquet upon his own account, urged the Duchess to injure him in the estimation of the Queen-mother; upon which Madame de Chevreuse, whose love of intrigue we have already mentioned, at once invited Anne of Austria to visit her at Dampierre, where she was met by Le Tellier and Colbert, and it was there arranged that she should ascertain, if possible, the feeling of her son towards the offending Minister.

As for some time past the King had refused to grant every favour solicited by the Queen-mother, he was delighted, on the present occasion, to appear as if con-

vinced by her arguments upon a point long decided
in his own mind, and it was soon resolved between
them that the Superintendent should be arrested; but
as he had a strong party in Paris, it was not deemed
prudent to attempt his seizure in the Capital, and a
journey to Nantes was ultimately determined on, in
order that Fouquet might be made prisoner in that
city, at the same time that the island of Belleisle, which
the Minister had lately purchased, and which he was
reported to be at that moment engaged in fortifying,
should be taken possession of in the King's name.

Louis XIV. had, even from the very appointment
of Fouquet, looked upon him with an unfavourable
eye.   We have already mentioned that during the life
of Mazarin he rendered the Sovereign more dependent
than ever upon his Eminence, by compelling him to
submit to the mortification of receiving, as a loan at
his hands, the sums necessary to his ordinary expenditure, which should at once have been delivered to him
by the Superintendent himself.   Nor was the feeling
of distrust lessened by the dying words of the Cardinal,
who, while he expatiated to his Royal master upon the
official talents of Fouquet, at the same time warned him
against his cupidity and licentiousness, which were
rendered only the more obnoxious by the intemperate
conduct of the abbé his brother, who, although he did
not scruple to profit by his relationship to the profligate
Minister, nevertheless exposed his vices and betrayed
his confidence.

The King acted in this emergency with both wisdom
and indulgence.   He took an early opportunity of
informing Fouquet that he was aware of his extortions,

and the uses to which he had applied their proceeds ; but declared that he was willing to forget the past, and to retain him in office, provided he were disposed to do his duty with fidelity for the future; that he was resolved to ascertain the state of the public finances, as the most important feature of his government; and that as Fouquet was the only person who could afford him the necessary information, he entreated him to do so without disguise or subterfuge; assuring him, moreover, that he would find it difficult to deceive him, and that any such attempt would inevitably subject him to the most condign disgrace.

Somewhat startled by such an address, the Superintendent had no sooner returned home than he consulted some of his friends as to the most prudent steps which he could adopt under circumstances so stringent, when they unanimously advised him to profit by the warning of the King, who had been forbearing enough to leave him an opportunity of retrieving himself while it was yet time; but Fouquet, after having listened to their arguments, still remained of a different opinion. He could not bring himself to believe that a young Sovereign of three-and-twenty would willingly imprison himself in his cabinet for hours together, day after day, in order to examine dry reports and intricate calculations, when he could command pleasure and festivity without. He entertained no doubt that Louis would become disgusted by so arid an occupation long before he had obtained one glimpse through the complicated labyrinth ; and even should it prove otherwise, Fouquet still flattered himself that he should find it an easy task to mystify and mislead a mere novice, and to compel him to renounce his undertaking, more than ever impressed with his dependence upon a Minister able enough to regulate the movements of so stupendous a piece of machinery.

It is more than probable that the crafty Superintendent would, in fact, have succeeded in his purpose, had not the King secretly confided to Colbert every evening the returns and reports furnished to him daily by Fouquet, which the young Secretary was employed throughout the night in examining with untiring zeal, in order that he might be enabled to point out their errors, and to explain their perfidy. He laid bare before the King alike the exaggerations and deficiencies which were necessary to blind him to the extent of the rapine committed on his treasury; and, on the morrow, Louis addressed such observations to the Superintendent as were calculated to convince him that he did not for a moment lose sight of his object, his aim being, if possible, to induce him to act with sincerity, although he soon lost all hope of being enabled to accomplish so desirable an object.*

Thus had several months elapsed, Fouquet striving to deceive, Louis appearing to be deceived, and Colbert preventing him from being so, when the insult offered to Mademoiselle de la Vallière, and the representations of the Queen-mother, determined the King to rid himself of so dishonest a Minister; and we have shown the precaution which it was considered necessary to take in order to accomplish this end.

Fouquet had so long held sole control over the finances of the kingdom, and had been so little scrupu-

* Louis XIV., sa Cour, et le Régent.

lous in its expenditure, that there was scarcely an individual of the Court who had not received from him either a present or a pension; he was said to have numerous partisans in Brittany, his birthplace, so zealous in his cause that they could raise all Provence at his slightest bidding ; while the Island of Belleisle was represented as his intended retreat should he ever incur the displeasure of the King, where, secure within his bristling walls and guarded ramparts, he might either defy the Royal power or deliver the Island to the English, as the price of an asylum in that country.

It was, consequently, not surprising that the King should be anxious to avoid all chance of failure in his attempt to secure the person of the Superintendent, who, although his subject, had, in a great degree, emancipated himself from his authority by his own precautions ; and the first step upon which he resolved was that of marching troops into Brittany, on the pretext of certain seditious movements, in consequence of a demand which he had made that the province should raise a sum of money as a gratuitous gift to the Crown, and the next that of proceeding there himself, and of causing Fouquet to bear him company.

The Superintendent was, at the moment when this proposition was made to him, suffering from an attack of fever ; but he made no plea of illness, being anxious to let the King see and understand the extent of his influence in Brittany, feeling convinced that it would secure to him the twofold advantage of throwing Colbert into the background, and of impressing upon Louis the importance of his own support.

Still it would appear that Fouquet was not altogether

free from apprehension; for on the arrival of the august party at Nantes, which was the term of the journey, he established himself in a residence at the extreme end of the town, whence, as it was afterwards ascertained, a subterranean passage opened upon the Loire, where a boat, thoroughly equipped, victualed, and provided with excellent rowers capable of overcoming all obstacles, was prepared to transport him, on any alarm, to Belleisle.

He had, moreover, caused couriers to be posted at different stations on the highroad, with relays so disposed, that, without being either seen or prevented, he could gain whatever place of safety he might select. Nevertheless, it is equally certain that he did not apprehend immediate danger, as he declared that he confided in the King, who was aware that during the lifetime of Mazarin he had acted on many occasions in obedience to the express orders of that Minister, while, in what had subsequently occurred, he had been sincere and faithful; and the King had appeared so satisfied with his explication that he firmly believed he had nothing to fear.

Rocking himself in this delusion, he was unguarded enough to invite Louis and all his Court to a fête at his chateau at Vaux, upon which he had expended the enormous sum of fifteen millions.* No step could

* The palace of Vaux le Vicomte, now called Vaux-Praslin, or, simply, Praslin, is a dependence of Maincy, a small village about a league from Melun. When purchased by Fouquet it was merely an obscure seigneurial residence; and a short time after his disgrace it became the property of Marshal Villars, and thence received the name of Vaux Villars. The son of the Marshal suffered the ornamental water to run to waste, destroyed the gardens, and finally sold the estate to the Duke of Praslin, from whom it derived its new alias, and in whose family it

have been more weak or ill-advised; for the King was little likely to forget, as he looked upon the splendour of Vaux (by which that of Fontainebleau and St. Germain was utterly eclipsed), that its owner had derived all his wealth from the public coffers, and that it had been accumulating at a period when he was himself in need of the funds which had here been so profusely lavished.

Every one who bore a distinguished name in France was bidden to this princely festival, which was destined to be commemorated by La Fontaine and Benserade, and where a prologue by Pélisson* was to be spoken, and a comedy by Molière to be played. The King arrived at the chateau, accompanied by an escort of musketeers, and was received at the gates by his imprudent host, who had no sooner welcomed him than he entered the park, followed by the whole Court, and found himself surrounded by a scene of enchantment, for which, despite all that he had heard of the gorgeous palace of his Minister, he was still far from being pre-

---

still remains. It is surrounded by a moat filled with running water; the great entrance-court is ornamented with porticoes, the subordinate buildings are spacious and magnificent, and the paintings which decorate the apartments in excellent preservation. The park is of considerable extent.

* Paul Pelisson Tontanier was a native of Béziers, and was born in 1624. He was the descendant of a Protestant family long distinguished in the legal profession. He fixed his residence in Paris in 1652, and purchased the charge of Royal Secretary; became a State Councillor in 1660, and head clerk of Fouquet, of whom he shared all the fortunes. When imprisoned in the Bastille he compiled, in defense of his friend, three Memorials, which are considered to be masterpieces of judicial eloquence, and monuments of the most unalterable friendship. After a captivity of five years he was liberated by order of Louis XIV., who honoured his consistency, and appointed him historiographer to the Crown. In 1693 he died, a member of the French Academy.

pared. A cloud passed over his brow, and the smile was very bitter with which he turned towards Fouquet, and remarked, " I shall never again, sir, venture to invite you to visit me; you would find yourself inconvenienced."

The epigram was too pointed to fail in its effect, and for a moment Fouquet turned pale; but he soon rallied, and persisted in doing the honours of his sumptuous home to the mortified Sovereign, with an ostentatious detail which left no one of its marvels unremarked.

The first surprise was the sudden play of the fountains, a luxury at that period almost unknown in France, where a solitary attempt of this description had been made by Henry IV. at St. Germain. The astonished admiration of the spectators may therefore be imagined, when it is stated that the Superintendent had purchased and pulled down three villages, in order that the water by which they were supplied might be conducted, from a distance of five leagues in every direction, into vast reservoirs of marble, manufactured in Italy.

As twilight deepened, the waters suddenly ceased their play, and a splendid banquet supervened; after which the *Fâcheux* of Molière was represented, and succeeded by a splendid pyrotechnic display; while the ball, which terminated the amusements, was protracted until daylight. Before its commencement Louis made a tour of the chateau, accompanied by its owner, and was compelled to acknowledge that nothing, in all probability, existed throughout Europe which could compete with it in magnificence.

During the ball Mademoiselle de la Vallière, having

danced several *courantes* with the King, became fatigued by the noise and excitement, and expressed a wish to retire for a time from the saloon; upon which Louis, drawing her arm through his, led her, in her turn, through the splendid suite of rooms by which he had been at once astonished and offended, and bade her remark the ostentation with which M. Fouquet had introduced his armorial bearings on all sides, and in every compartment of the ceilings. The shield bore a squirrel, with the motto, *Quô non ascendam?* and, as she was engaged in reading it, Colbert chanced to enter the apartment, of whom she inquired its meaning.

"It signifies, ' To what height may I not attain?' madam; and it is understood by those who know the boldness of the squirrel, or that of his master," replied the Secretary, with marked emphasis.

Louis bit his lip.

At that particular moment M. Pélisson chanced to pass, and overhearing the rejoinder, he remarked, with a profound bow, as he fixed his eyes steadily upon Colbert, while he addressed the King, " Your Majesty has probably not remarked that, in every instance, the squirrel is pursued by an adder;" and then, with a second salutation, he disappeared.

Colbert turned pale and his eyes flashed, while the anger of the King was so violent that he desired the Captain of his musketeers might be instantly ordered to attend him.

Mademoiselle de la Vallière, who understood only too well the meaning of this summons, immediately threw herself at his feet, and entreated that he would

not compromise his dignity by arresting a man who
was his host, whatever might be his crime, or terminate
a fête, given in his own honour, by making it the
medium of an act of violence. Fortunately, she at
the moment caught sight of the Queen-mother, who
was entering a lateral apartment, and hastily springing
from her knees, she hurried to inform her of the
King's intentions, and besought her interference. Not
a moment was lost; and with considerable difficulty
Louis was at length induced to delay his vengeance, and
to return to Fontainebleau, only in part consoled for the
humiliation to which he had been subjected by a firm
determination that the insult should never be repeated.

A fortnight after the ill-omened fête at Vaux, the
Court proceeded to Nantes, the King pretexting the
state of his health, and his anxiety to show so fine a
city to the Queen. He was preceded by the three
Ministers—Fouquet and his friend Lionne in one barge
impelled by eight rowers, and Colbert in a second
similarly provided; and as they passed along the river,
each endeavouring to pass the other, a courtier remarked that one of the two would suffer shipwreck at
Nantes. The King arrived on the following day, having travelled post, attended by several of his confidential friends, among whom was the Marquis de
Péguilain, whose fever continued undiminished, and
his first question was if Le Tellier had preceded him.
On being answered in the affirmative, he desired that
inquiries might be made as to the health of M. Fouquet, whose fever had augmented, and how he had
borne the journey, as he wished to see him in the
course of the day.

The messenger, however, met the Superintendent on his way to his castle of Nantes to pay his respects to his Majesty; but on the morrow the same ceremony was observed, when M. de Brienne found him much worse in health, but in high spirits; and after he had acquitted himself of his embassy, and was taking his leave, the invalid inquired, in a cheerful tone, what were the news at Court.

" That you are about to be arrested," was the reply.

" You are misinformed, my good friend," said Fouquet, with a smile; " it is Colbert who is about to be arrested, and not myself."

" Are you sure of this ? " asked Brienne.

" Perfectly; for it was I who gave the order for him to be conducted to the castle of Angers, and it was Pélisson who paid the workmen intrusted to place the prison beyond all chance of successful assault."

On his return, Louis XIV. questioned the young Secretary very minutely with regard to the health of the Superintendent, who was attacked by his malady on alternate days; but his manner convinced Brienne that the Minister was lost, as, in speaking of him, the King no longer styled him M. Fouquet, but simply Fouquet; and when he was at length dismissed, Louis desired him to be in attendance at an early hour on the following morning, and to bring Fouquet with him, as he was going to hunt.

He was, however, again anticipated by the Superintendent, who having been informed that the King desired to see him before he left the castle, was in attendance at six o'clock, little suspecting that all was prepared for his arrest; and, after a conference of half an hour, he was returning quietly through the gallery, when he was met by M. de la Feuillade,* who told him in a low voice to be cautious, as orders had been issued against him.

For the first time Fouquet began to quail, as he could not conceal from himself that the manner of the King had been constrained and absent; and this fact, coupled with the hint of the Duke, induced him, when he gained the courtyard, to throw himself into the carriage of one of his friends, instead of his own, with the intention of making his escape. He had already succeeded in passing the gates and entering the town, when Artagnan, who commanded the musketeers, and to whom his arrest had been intrusted, seized him as he was about to turn into a lateral street, transferred him to his own coach, and conveyed him, without stopping either day or night, to the castle of Angers, which he had caused to be prepared for the reception of Colbert; and thus this modern Haman found that the pains which he had taken to strengthen the external fortifications of the prison only rendered his own prospect of escape utterly hopeless. His wife and children were at the same time removed to Limoges,

---

* Francis of Aubusson, Duke of la Feuillade, was a descendant of the Dukes of Aubusson; served under Louis XIV., and became a Marshal of France and Colonel of the French Guards. In 1664 he commanded the French forces at the battle of St. Gothard, and was created Duke of Roanne. In 1668 he went to the relief of Candia, then besieged by Achmet-Kioperli. He made the campaign of Holland; followed the King in Franche-Comté, and terminated the conquest of that province by the capture of Dôle, Salins, etc. In 1676 he commanded the army in Flanders; and in 1678 he was at the head of the navy. In 1691 he obtained the Government of Dauphiny, and ultimately died in 1681. He erected, at his own expense, a statue of Louis XIV., in the *Place des Victoires*.

and seals placed upon all his property; while an attendant, who was present at his arrest, hastened to secure one of the private relays which had been prepared
in case of emergency, and made the journey to Paris
with such speed that the news of his capture was known
to all the friends of the fallen Minister twelve hours
before the arrival of the courier despatched to the
Queen-mother.

During this interval many of Fouquet's papers might
have been secured, especially in his house at St. Mande,
where he had deposited a vast number; and the abbé,
his brother, suggested that, without delaying to examine them, they should at once be collected and burned
to the last fragment, declaring that the value of what
would be thus destroyed on the one hand would bear
no proportion to the benefit of that which would be
annihilated on the other.   Madame Duplessis-Bellièvre,
however, who was the fast friend and confidante of the
Minister, objected to so extreme a measure, feeling
convinced that, in the anxiety of mind which he had
lately suffered, he could not have failed to obliterate
everything which might injure either himself or others.   She was, however, unfortunately mistaken.   The
Superintendent was in the habit of preserving every
communication which he received, whatever might be
its nature—proposals, requests, acknowledgments, prop-
ositions, billets-doux; nothing was destroyed; and the
result of such a system, pursued by such a man as
Fouquet, may be readily understood.   All these multitudinous papers were rigidly examined by the King
and the Queen-mother; and a great and well-founded
terror spread through the Court when this fact was

ascertained; for numerous were the hitherto fair and noble names which were destined to be forever sullied by the disclosures they contained.

Few there were, either married or single, says Madame de Motteville, who had not sacrificed to the golden calf; and it was proved that the poets well understood their vocation when they wrote the fable of Danaë and the Shower of Gold.

After the arrest of Fouquet the Royal party had immediately returned to Fontainebleau; and while the examinations were pending, all his friends became greatly alarmed for the result; and the rather as being principally artists and men of letters, without any interest at Court, they were unable to make an effort in his behalf. It was soon rumoured that among his female correspondents the Superintendent had numbered Madame de Sévigné, whose letters had, like the rest, passed through the hands of the King; and more than one of those who knew themselves to be compromised rejoiced at the idea of being partially excused by the companionship of this hitherto irreproachable name. Their triumph was, however, of short duration.

The life of Madame de Sévigné, despite the buoyancy of heart which she retained until her death, had been one of suffering and difficulty. Married in youth to a profligate, who eventually lost his life in a duel, disgraceful to his memory both as a husband and a father—a widow at five-and-twenty, agreeable in person and accomplished in mind, Madame de Sévigné had withstood every temptation to a second alliance, devoting herself to the care and education of her chil-

dren with a tenderness and perseverance perfectly exemplary; while that she did not meet with all the support and encouragement from her own family which
she might justly have claimed under these circumstances, is sufficiently evident from a letter addressed
to her by her cousin, Bussy-Rabutin, so early as the
year 1654, in which that shallow-hearted and libertine
nobleman, who was aware that both Fouquet and the
Prince de Conti had made dishonourable advances to
Madame de Sévigné, and who feared that from her
continued resistance they would become wearied of
their pursuit, attacked her by arguments as disgraceful
as they were revolting, in order to induce her to comply with their proposals.

He did not, however, estimate at its just value the
noble nature which he strove to abase. The wages of
immorality had no attraction in the eyes of Madame
de Sévignê. Her path of duty lay well defined before
her, and the thorns and briers by which it was beset
she was content to pluck away as she advanced,
strengthened in the heaviest hour of her toil by the
aid of an approving conscience.

It was stated that both Anne of Austria and her son
were startled when the signature of Marie Rabutin
Chantal met their eyes; but their consternation was
not of long continuance; while the subject of her
communication, and her own perfect and womanly
feelings on learning the discovery of her letters among
the private papers of Fouquet, are admirably developed
in the following note to M. de Pomponne: *

---

* Simon Arnauld, Marquis de Pomponne, afterwards Minister for
Foreign Affairs.

"At the Rocks, this 11th Oct., 1661.

" There is nothing more true than that friendship becomes more warm when people are interested in the same subject; you have so obligingly written to me to that effect, that I can make you no better reply than by the assurance that I have the same sentiments towards yourself which you entertain for me; and that, in one word, I both honour and esteem you in a high degree.   But what say you of all that has been found in these caskets?   Should you ever have believed that my poor letters, full of the marriage of M. de la Trousse, and all the affairs of his family, would have been discovered so mysteriously situated?   I assure you that, whatever credit I may derive from those who do me justice for having had with him no other commerce than this, I am nevertheless painfully wounded to find that I am compelled to justify myself, and perhaps very uselessly, towards a thousand people who will never comprehend the fact.   I think that you will easily understand the grief caused by such a necessity to a heart like mine.   I beseech you to say all you know upon this point; I cannot have friends enough upon such an occasion." *

Strong in her innocence, Madame de Sévigné did not, consequently, hesitate to accompany Mademoiselle de Scudéry,† when she declared her intention of

---

* Lettres de Madame de Sévign

† Madelaine de Scudéry was born at Havre, in 1607, and went at an early age to Paris, where she became an authoress, from necessity: a fact which did not, however, militate against her admission to the best society, while her wit made her a welcome addition to all the literary circles of the time.   Her novels are numerous, and obtained great success, although they are wanting in nature, and essentially French as regards the persons described.   Her principal works are

waiting upon La Vallière, to solicit her interest in favour of the condemned Minister; and they found a willing Coadjutor in the gentle Louise, who was as anxious to preserve the life of Fouquet as the warmest of his friends, and who exerted all her influence over the mind of the King to induce his mercy: an attempt in which, seconded by the Queen-mother (who, amid all her indignation, was desirous that he should not suffer the extreme penalty of his offences), she happily succeeded.

Cyrus, Clelia, Ibrahim, Matilda of Aquilar, Almahida, Celanira, etc. She died in 1701.

CHAPTER VI

THE pleasures of Fontainebleau soon effaced all memory of the imprisoned Superintendent; and the birth of a Dauphin, which took place on the

Louis XIV. Everything by which he could be affected appeared subject to the influence of his will: the treaty of the Pyrenees had terminated a long and exhausting war; Mazarin, by whose authority he had been oppressed, was in his grave; Fouquet, by whom he had been rivalled in the magnificence upon which he prided himself, was his prisoner; the Queen, to whom he was indifferent, had given him an heir to the throne; and Mademoiselle de la Vallière, whom he loved, already began to resist less steadily the encroachments of his passion; while the religious struggle, which was fated to recommence hereafter was for the moment appeased by the dispossession of the Calvinists of all the privileges which the Edict of Nantes was intended to secure to them, and who only continued their opposition through the medium of a secret system of proselytism, destined on a future day to convulse once more the whole face of the kingdom. This was, moreover, so cautiously pursued, that no suspicion of its extent disturbed, even for a moment, the apparent calm; and Louis, satisfied that he had at length accomplished a general pacification which he should be enabled to maintain, resigned himself wholly to a career of pleasure.

Every festival had Mademoiselle de la Vallière for its object; and although it professed to have no view save that of gratifying the Queen, it was not only a homage offered by the King to the reigning favourite, but it also conduced to the aggrandisement of royalty, by weakening the resources of that haughty nobility which, since the reign of Francis II., had perpetually disturbed the repose of France; for, in order to com-

pete with the magnificence of the Monarch, the greater
portion of those around him mortgaged and even dissipated their patrimony, and, when these measures
were no longer practicable, became involved in debt;
and, once ruined, found themselves entirely dependent
upon the Sovereign; while the extraordinary number
of foreigners who were attracted to Paris by the perpetual fêtes produced a revenue from the customs
which exceeded that disbursed by the treasury.   It
was during this period that the famous tilting-match
took place in the Place Royale, to which it gave the
name that it still bears.

Throughout the whole of the winter the Court continued immersed in pleasure, and several ballets were
produced, in which the King bore a conspicuous part,
seeking so little to disguise his passion for La Vallière
that he was careful every evening to ascertain the
colours she would wear on the morrow, in order that he
might appear in the same.   In order, also, to excite
her to greater display of magnificence, he overwhelmed
her with jewels and costly dresses; but she shrunk so
resolutely from all which could tend to make her conspicuous, that he could not induce her to abandon the
simplicity in which she gloried to perceive that she
was equally attractive in his eyes.

On one occasion the King had joined the evening
circle of *Madame*, and was, according to his usual
habit, conversing with her fair maid of honour, when
some despatches were delivered to him which were declared to be of immediate importance. He accordingly seated himself near a table to examine them,
and it was soon remarked by every one that his

cheek became blanched, and that he bit his lips with a violence which indicated suppressed passion. Nevertheless, not a word escaped him until he had read them to an end, when he rose, and crushing the despatches convulsively between his fingers, exclaimed, haughtily,

"Here are news for you, gentlemen! Our Ambassador in London has been publicly insulted by the Spanish Envoy. What think you of this, gentlemen? Shall I wait to revenge the insult of my father-in-law until my moustache is as long as his own? He, without doubt, imagines that we are still under the guardianship of the Cardinal. M. le Tellier, let my Ambassador at Madrid leave that city instantly, and the Spanish Envoy quit Paris within four-and-twenty hours. The conferences of Flanders are at an end; and if the superiority of our crown is not recognised publicly by Spain, she may hold herself prepared to renew the war."

The consternation excited by these words will admit of no description, and even Le Tellier hesitated for a moment as though he doubted the evidence of his senses; but he was soon undeceived by Louis, who, in a still higher tone, demanded if he had not understood his orders, desiring him, at the same time, to assemble the Council, at which he would preside within an hour.

This done, the King once more approached the ladies who were present, and continued the conversation which had been so unpleasantly interrupted, as calmly as though nothing had occurred to ruffle his temper. The affront he had received was, neverthe-

less, of a very serious character, and one to which,
constituted as he was, he could not fail to be susceptible. An Ambassador from Sweden had arrived in
England, and, on his entrance, the Count of Estrade,
the French representative, and the Baron de Vateville,
the representative of Spain, had disputed a point of
precedence. The Spaniard, by a greater profusion
and a more numerous retinue, had gained over the
populace; and having caused the horses which drew
the carriages of M. d'Estrade to be killed, and his attendants wounded and dispersed, the Spaniards had
taken possession of the contested right without sheath-
ing their swords.

The orders of Louis XIV. were obeyed. M. d'Estrade was recalled; the Baron de Vateville dismissed
the kingdom; and the conferences which were still in
progress in Flanders, on the subject of the limits of the
respective nations, were suddenly terminated; while a
message was despatched from the French King to
Philip IV. to inform him that if he did not immediately recognise the supremacy of his Crown, and repair the insult to which it had been subjected, by a
formal apology, the peace was at an end.

The Spanish Sovereign, who was unwilling to plunge
his kingdom once more into bloodshed for so insignificant a consideration as the precedence of an Ambassador, consented to heal the wounded pride of his
tenacious son-in-law; and, accordingly, on the 24th
March, 1662, the Count of Fuentes waited upon the
offended Monarch at Fontainebleau, where, in the
presence of all the foreign Ministers then resident at
the Court of France, he declared, in the name of his

Royal master, that thenceforward the Spanish Ambassadors should never again compete with those of France: a concession which, if it did not altogether admit the preeminence of Louis, at least betrayed the weakness of Spain.*

Scarcely had this trifling affair been settled in a manner which redounded so greatly to the honour of the French King than he found himself called upon to decide another of a similar description, but in which he was less personally interested. The Duke of Créqui,† who was Ambassador at Rome, had revolted the Roman people, and still more the Roman nobility, by his overweening haughtiness, and had, consequently, become eminently unpopular; while his servants, exaggerating his error, had committed many excesses, even proceeding so far as to attack the night-watch of the city; and, upon one occasion, some of his lackeys amused themselves by charging a squadron of the Pope's Corsican guard, sword in hand, and putting them to flight.

The whole corps, incensed, and privately encouraged by Don Mario Chigi, the brother of Alexander VII., who detested the Duke of Crequi, assembled in arms round the residence of the Ambassador, and fired upon

---

* Louis XIV. et son Siècle. *Francheville.*

† Charles de Créqui, de Blanchefort, et de Canaples, Prince de Poix, Governor of Dauphiny, peer and Marshal of France, became Duke of Lesdiguières by his marriage with Madelaine de Bonne, daughter of the celebrated Connétable de Lesdiguières. His duel with Don Philippin, the bastard of Savoy, on the subject of a scarf, in which he killed his antagonist, contributed, in no small degree, to establish his reputation. He took Pignerol and La Maurienne in 1630, was sent Ambassador to Rome in 1633, defeated the Spanish forces at the battle of Tésin, in 1636, and was killed by a cannon-ball at the siege of Bremen.

the carriage of the Duchess as she was in the act of
alighting, killing a page, and wounding several of her
attendants; upon which M. de Créqui immediately
left Rome, accusing the relatives of the Pope, and
even the Pope himself, of having sanctioned the as-
sassination. Alexander delayed, as long as he was
able to do so, any offer of reparation, having so little
opinion of the steadiness of the French as to believe
that if he temporised they would soon forget their
annoyance; but, finally, he caused one of the Corsicans
and a Constable to be hanged at the end of four
months, and banished the Governor of the city, who
was suspected of having authorised the outrage. He
was, however, compelled to more definite measures by
the intelligence that Louis XIV. threatened to besiege
Rome, that he was already landing troops in Italy, and
that the command had been given to the Marshal of
Plessis-Praslin.* The affair had become a national
quarrel, and the King of France was evidently resolved
that it should involve no dishonour to his own kingdom; while the Pope, on his side, was equally determined not to yield so long as he possessed one hope
of overcoming his adversary, and, accordingly, he
supplicated the mediation of all the Roman Catholic
Princes; but the Holy Father had fallen upon evil
times: Germany was threatened by the Turks, and
Spain was hampered by an unsuccessful war against
Portugal.

* Cæsar de Choiseuil du Plessis-Praslin, Duke and peer of France,
was created Marshal of France in 1645, and in 1648 won the battle of
Francheron, and in 1650 that of Réthel against Marshal Turenne, who
at that period commanded the Spanish army. He died in Paris in
1673, at the advanced age of seventy-eight years.

The Roman Court, consequently, only irritated Louis, without having it in its power to injure him; while the Parliament of Provence cited the Pope and seized the *comtat* of Avignon.   In earlier times an ex-communication from Rome would have been the immediate result of so decided a proceeding; but such an expedient had now ceased to be available, and would only have excited ridicule.   Thus the Head of the Church found himself compelled to bend to circumstances, to exile his own brother from Rome, and to announce his intention of sending his nephew, as *legate à latere*, to France, to offer satisfaction to the offended dignity of its Monarch.*

Shortly after this event the unfortunate La Vallière sacrificed her reputation to her ardent passion for the King; but her remorse was so great, that, far from parading her disgrace, as most of those around her would have done, she was so prostrated by shame as to absent herself, so far as her Court duties would permit, from all society; and the agony of her repentance was so violent as to occasion much embarrassment to her Royal lover; while the reproaches of the Queen-mother, and the deep melancholy of Maria Theresa, added to his annoyance.   The young Queen had reluctantly admitted the conviction of this new misfortune; but two incidents soon occurred which robbed her even of the equivocal happiness of doubt.

A young valet-de-chambre of the King, named Belloc, had invented a species of interlude, consisting of dialogues interspersed with dances, which obtained great favour at Court, where they were enacted by all

* Siècle de Louis XIV.

the principal persons of the Royal circle, including Louis himself. On a particular occasion one of these interludes, of which the subject had been prompted by the King, was represented in the Queen's apartments; and the boldness with which it shadowed forth the love of the Monarch for La Vallière was so great that, long ere its conclusion, a score of whispers had identified the characters, and she herself retired to her chamber, trembling at its probable effect upon those whom it was so well calculated to wound.

A few days only passed over ere she was summoned to the presence of the Queen-mother, and the circumstance was so unusual that Louise hesitated whether she should obey without previously consulting the King. A second messenger, however, urging her to hasten, left her no alternative; and with a sinking heart she was ushered into the apartment of Anne of Austria, whom she found closeted with *Madame*. There was an expression of triumph playing about the lip of the Princess which at once convinced Mademoiselle de la Vallière that she was summoned on no indifferent subject, and one glance at the clouded brow of the Queen-mother confirmed her in her conviction. Her fears had not outrun the truth. Coldly, haughtily, and peremptorily, Anne of Austria declared her dismission from the Court, adding that she was immediately to return whence she came, and that Madame de Choisy would conduct her to her home.

With a trembling heart La Vallière attempted to inquire the nature of her offence; but Anne of Austria indignantly interposed, saying that it sufficed that there could not be two Queens of France; after which she rose, and, followed by *Madame*, retired to an inner apartment.

The unhappy girl staggered back to her room almost unconsciously. A full conviction of the disgrace which she had brought upon herself bowed her to the dust. She was about to be ignominiously driven from the Court, to meet her mother as a guilty and condemned wretch, to whom the whole world was now only one wide desolation; while, at intervals, the idea that she was to be forever separated from the King dried her tears with the scorching fever of despair. No one intruded upon her solitude throughout the day, and she gave a free course to the anguish by which she was oppressed; but with the twilight Louis entered her apartment, and, finding her exhausted with weeping, insisted on learning the cause of her distress. Anxious though she was that he should know all, she shrunk from exciting the storm which she was well aware must follow, and she persisted in withholding her secret, despite the entreaties, reproaches, and even threats of the King, who eventually, displeased by her pertinacity, rose from her side, and without uttering another word, left the room.

As he disappeared, Mademoiselle de la Vallière sunk back tearless and hopeless. She was now, indeed, alone; for even he for whom she had suffered had abandoned her, and hours went by before she again ventured to lift her head. After a time, however, she remembered that a compact had once been made between herself and her Royal lover, that, in the event of any misunderstanding, a night should not be suffered to elapse without a reconciliation. Her heart

again beat more freely. He would not fail her; he
could not forget his promise—he would write to tell
her that his anger against her was at an end. And so
she waited and watched, and counted every hour as it
was proclaimed by the belfry of the palace; but she
waited and watched in vain ; and when at length, after
this long and weary night, the daylight streamed
through the silken curtains of her chamber, she threw
herself upon her knees, and praying that God would
not cast away the victim who was thus rejected by the
world, she hastened with a burning cheek and a tearless eye to collect a few necessary articles of clothing,
and throwing on her veil and mantle, rushed down a
private staircase, and escaped into the street. In this
distracted state of mind she pursued her way to
Chaillot, and reached the convent of the Sisters of St.
Mary, where she was detained for a considerable time
in the parlour; but at length the grating was opened,
and a portress appeared, who, on her request to be
admitted to the abbess, informed her that all the community were at their devotions, and could not be seen
by any one.

It was in vain that the poor fugitive entreated, and
asserted her intention of taking the vows; she could
extort no other answer; and the portress withdrew,
leaving her sitting upon a wooden bench, desolate and
heartstruck. For two hours she remained motionless,
with her eyes fixed upon the grating, but it continued
closed; even the dreary refuge of this poor and obscure
convent was denied to her—even the house of religion
had barred its doors against her. She could bear up
no longer; from the previous morning she had not

tasted food; and the fatigue of body and anguish of mind which she had undergone, combined with this unaccustomed fast, had exhausted her slight remains of strength: a sullen torpor gradually overcame her faculties, and eventually she fell upon the paved floor, cold and insensible.

Early in the morning the King was informed of the disappearance of Mademoiselle de la Vallière; and he had no sooner learned the fact than he hastened to the Tuileries to question *Madame,* who either was, or affected to be, utterly ignorant of her fate. Nor was he more fortunate in his inquiries of the Queen-mother, who, while she declared her inability to give him the information that he sought, reproached him with his want of self-command, remarking that he had no mastery over himself.

" It may be so," he exclaimed, goaded by her words; " but if I cannot control myself, I shall at least know how to control those who outrage me."

As yet he had obtained no clew to the retreat of his mistress; but Louis was not to be discouraged, and he adopted such efficient measures as, ere long, led him to a knowledge of the convent to which the unhappy fugitive had been seen to bend her steps. In another instant he was on horseback, and, followed by a single page, galloped off in the direction of Chaillot, where, as no warning had been given of his approach, the grating remained inhospitably closed, and he found the wretched girl still stretched on the pavement.

It was long ere Louise was aware whose tears were falling fast upon her face, and whose hands had clasped her own. After a time, however, she recognised the

King, and at length was enabled to confide to him the reason of her flight, and to implore him to leave her free to fulfil the resolution she had formed ; but Louis was deaf to her entreaties, and finally succeeded in inducing her to pardon the past, and to return. It was not without compunction that she suffered herself to be persuaded, but her passion for the King ultimately triumphed over her scruples ; and the page was despatched for a carriage, in which, bathed in tears, half joy, half bitterness, she reached Paris, and once more found herself under the roof of that palace which, only a few hours previously, she believed that she had quitted forever.

It was with considerable difficulty that the King prevailed upon *Madame* to restore to Mademoiselle de la Vallière the place in her household from which she had been so abruptly dismissed; but he was firm in his determination ; and eventually, although with a reluctance which she made no attempt to disguise, she consented to his wishes ; when, regardless of the manner of the concession, Louis thanked her for her compliance, and hastened to inform the anxious maid of honour of the success of his suit.

A short time subsequently, the Duke of Bouillon became the husband of Marianne de Mancini, the only niece whom the Cardinal had left unmarried; but this alliance created little sensation at court. Madame de Soissons gave a supper on the occasion, at which the Queen consented to appear; and then the affair was forgotten.

Meanwhile, Louis had never overcome the mortification to which he had been subjected at Vaux, and the

determination which he had then formed to construct
for himself a palace, of which the splendour should
be unapproachable by any subject, whatever might be
his resources. He resolved not to build only for the
age, but for futurity; and after considerable hesitation,
he at length fixed upon the park of Versailles as its
site.* Louis XIII., whose hunting-parties frequently
took place in the forest of Versailles, and who, on one
occasion, overtaken by the darkness near a small ele-
vation above the road leading to St. Leger, was compelled to pass the night in a mill, while his attendants
and the hounds were housed in the cottage of a
wagoner, caused a small pavilion, of which some traces
may still be seen in a street of the town, to be erected
for his future accommodation, should he again chance
to be benighted in that neighbourhood, and ultimately
purchased a sufficient extent of land to enable him to
erect a chateau, and to form a park in the centre of
the forest; when, having decided that the house should

---

* "Versailles possessed, as early as the 10th century, a fief and a
seigneurial manor, situated on the slope of the hill which overlooks
the wood of Satory, on the spot since covered by the labyrinth known
as the Queen's Grove; and labour had not yet lowered this soil, which
was on the same level as the sheet of water. Several large farms, acquired at different periods, extended the domain to the village of
Choisy-au-Beuf, which Louis XIV. inclosed in the great park. The
most ancient deed referring to Versailles bears the date of 1037.
. . . L'Etoile, in his *Memoirs* (vol. i. p. 26), asserts that Cath-
erine de Medicis caused the Secretary of State, Loménie, to be
strangled, in order that the Count of Retz might possess the chateau
of Versailles; but this fact is improbable. Anthony de Loménie, who
enjoyed the intimacy of Henry IV., could easily have obtained the
restitution of the domain, if it had been thus usurped; while, on the
contrary, it is well known that it was from the tutor of the children of
Martial de Loménie that Albert de Gondi purchased the chateau,
which was at the time in a state of ruin."—*Versailles Ancien et
Moderne.*

stand upon the rise then occupied by the windmill in which he had formerly taken shelter, he left his architect, Lemercier, at liberty to construct it according to his own taste.

The result was by no means commensurate with the dignity of its owner; for although the building was not devoid of a certain elegance, it was insignificant in size, and was styled, by St. Simon, a " pasteboard palace "; while Bassompierre asserts that it was a residence of which no nobleman would have had cause to feel vain.   Nor did Louis XIV., when he finally resolved to embellish Versailles, in all probability, contemplate the vast changes which were ultimately effected there; for, in the first instance, he made no outlay save upon the gardens, leaving the little palace precisely as it stood; in which state it still existed so late as in 1664, when he gave there those marvellous entertainments which became matter of European celebrity, and whose effect he had awaited before he resolved upon the great pecuniary sacrifice which a more extended undertaking must necessarily involve.

Le Nôtre, intrusted with the disposition of the gardens, profited by a moment of enthusiasm on the part of the King, while examining the plan which he proposed, and of a consent wrung from him with considerable difficulty, to cut down, during a single night, a great portion of the masses of ornamental timber which had been planted by Louis XIII.; and the magnificence of the result excused him in the eyes of his Royal master for having ventured to exceed his orders.

Mansard,* however, to whom the erection of the palace was confided, was less fortunate; for by no argument which he was able to adduce, could he prevail upon the Monarch to sanction the demolition of the *pasteboard palace*, which had been the chosen refuge of his father, when, offended by the haughtiness of Mary de Medicis towards the Cardinal, he sought to escape from becoming the witness of scenes which wounded alike his pride and his filial respect. In vain did Mansard represent, that by his persistence in preserving the chamber where he was born, the Cardinal de Richelieu had ruined the plan of the chateau which he had built; the King only smiled; and when the architect, as a last hope, dilated upon the bad condition of the present edifice, his reply was to the effect that, if it were found absolutely necessary to pull it down, he should not oppose the measure, but that it must be rebuilt precisely as it stood; and thus the unfortunate Mansard found himself without any alternative, save that of concealing as much as possible the obnoxious edifice by the regal pile which was about to rise around it.†

We have alluded, in this rapid sketch, to the magnificent fêtes given in the gardens of Versailles in

---

* Jules Hardouin Mansard, born in 1635, became first architect to the King, Knight of St. Michael, and Controller and Director-General of buildings, arts, and manufactures. It was after the designs of this famous architect that the gallery of the Palais-Royal, the Place Louis-le-Grand, and that des Victoires were constructed. He also built the dome of the Hôtel des Invalides, and planned the establishment of St. Cyr, the cascade of St. Cloud, the menagerie, orangery, and stables of the palace of Versailles, and built the Trianon. He was protecting member of the Royal academy of painting and sculpture, and died in 1708.

† Versailles Ancien et Moderne.

1664; but they were so remarkable as to merit more special mention, alike from their magnificence, their singularity, and their intellectual attractions, which added a new grace to the profuse splendour that was their main characteristic. Versailles had even then become a delightful residence, although it as yet betrayed no vestige of its after-greatness.

Early in the spring, the King, followed by a Court composed of six hundred individuals, the whole of whose personal expenses were defrayed, as well as those of their respective attendants, took up his abode at Versailles; and the marvellous rapidity with which his artificers erected the stages, amphitheatres, and porticoes, all elaborately ornamented, which were required in succession to give effect to the various entertainments, was not one of the least prodigies of the festival. The fêtes commenced by a *carrousel*, in which all those who were to compete appeared in review order on the previous day, preceded by heralds-at-arms, pages, and equerries, who bore their shields and devices, on the former of which were inscribed, in letters of gold, verses written for the occasion by Périgni and Benserade.

The King represented Roger; and all the crown jewels sparkled upon his dress and on the housing of his charger. The Queen, attended by three hundred ladies, seated under triumphal arches, were the spectators of the procession. The cavalcade was followed by a gilded car, eighteen feet in height, fifteen in width, and twenty-four in length, representing the chariot of the sun. The four ages of gold, silver, steel, and iron, the signs of the zodiac, the seasons, and

the hours, followed immediately behind it; while the lists were carried by shepherds, and adjusted amid flourishes of trumpets, contrasted at intervals by the music of bagpipes and violins.

When the tilting terminated, and twilight threatened to cause a cessation of the festivities, four thousand immense torches suddenly illuminated the space destined to the banquet; and the tables were served by two hundred attendants, habited as dryads, wood-deities, and fauns; in the midst of whom Pan and Diana approached the august circle on the summit of a moving mountain, whence they descended only to superintend the arrangement of a repast which combined all the luxuries attainable by art or expense. Behind the tables, which formed a vast crescent, an orchestra was suddenly erected as if by magic, and peopled with musicians; the arcades surrounding the banqueting-hall and theatre were lighted by five hundred girandoles of green and silver, and a gilt balustrade inclosed the whole of the immense area.

The fêtes lasted seven days, and the prizes prepared for the victors in the lists were most magnificent.*

On this occasion the *Princesse d'Elide* of Molière was produced in the presence of the Sovereign and the whole Court, and was succeeded, on a subsequent day, by the three first acts of the *Tartuffe*, upon which he had been engaged at intervals for several years. He was quite aware of the obstacles which must be overcome before it could appear upon the public stage; and in the hope of obtaining, in the first place, the powerful protection of Royal favour, he had urged

* Siècle de Louis XIV.

that he should be permitted to cause its representation at Versailles. He was not, however, fated to see the whole of his hope fulfilled; for he had not adopted the necessary precautions which might have insured the acceptance of ideas at once so bold and so novel as those which he had put forth in the *Tartuffe*. He had neglected to define the delicate shades by which piety and bigotry were to be distinguished; and thus the Court, although at that period much less scrupulous than it afterwards became, took offence; and the King, upon the grounds we have stated, forbade a repetition of the performance.

This order was a heavy blow to Molière; but nevertheless, feeling that in the *Tartuffe* he had presented his masterpiece, he would not permit himself altogether to despair; and, accordingly, during the next five years, he applied all his energies to its improvement, corrected all that was already written, and completed what was still wanting. For this purpose he made his studies in the varied society of the Capital, and became the censor rather of the looks and bearing of those about him than of their words. It is scarcely necessary to state that opportunities for such observation were not wanting; the interdict which had been pronounced against his work had, more than ever, excited interest in its author, and Molière became the fashion.*

At the close of 1664, having become convinced of the perfect eligibility of the site which had been chosen, Louis XIV. finally authorised the commencement of the stupendous work which was destined to

* Vie de Molière, par M. Petitot.

immortalise his name; and the foundations were laid of the palace of Versailles, fated, before its completion, to swallow up the enormous sum of one hundred and sixty-five millions, a hundred and thirty-one thousand, four hundred and ninety-four livres.

But this was by no means the only great undertaking accomplished by the French King at this period. In the solitude of the cabinet he concerted with Colbert most of those splendid measures which tended to illustrate his reign. Under the prompting of this far-sighted and zealous Minister, he encouraged men of letters, and founded the manufactories which were destined to render France a great commercial nation. Vessels were launched which suddenly rendered his naval strength respectable; a reinforcement was sent to the Emperor of Austria against the Turks; the Duke of Beaufort was intrusted with the command of the expedition of Gigeri, which was succeeded by that of Cyprus, where he was fated to perish; the Louvre was completed as the walls of Versailles began to rise above the soil; an Indian company was organised; and the manufacture of the Gobelins was purchased in the King's name; while, as regarded external relations, both Spain and Rome, which had ventured to contest his supremacy, were compelled to make reparation to the authority they had failed to recognise.

Nor must mention be omitted of the creation, at the same period, of no less than seventy Knights of the Holy Ghost, by Louis XIV., who, as a signal and unprecedented favour, left one nomination at the disposal of the Prince de Condé; and beside this national recompense, originated by Henry III., his descendant also instituted another for personal services, which, however puerile it must appear to posterity, was too characteristic of Louis, and too much sought after by the greatest nobles of the Court, to be passed over in silence.   This extraordinary distinction, which he retained the right of bestowing and withdrawing at his pleasure, was the privilege of wearing a blue outer-coat, embroidered with gold and silver, precisely similar to his own, and was accorded by a patent authorising the wearer to accompany the King in his hunting-parties and his drives.

From that moment his favourites, more fortunate than his soldiers, had a uniform by which they might be known; and Condé the Conqueror solicited and obtained the favour of donning this envied habit, not because he had gained half-a-dozen battles for France, but because he had efficiently played the courtier at Fontainebleau.*   It may be expedient to remark that these outer-coats were worn over vests ornamented with ribbons, and that above the coat was slung a shoulder-belt supporting a sword, while a throat-band of muslin, edged with fine lace, and a broad-brimmed beaver, surmounted by a double row of plumes, completed the costume, which continued in vogue until 1684, and became the fashion throughout all Europe, with the exception of Spain and Poland.

Meanwhile, the position of Mademoiselle de Vallière was far from being a happy one; for, superadded to the remorse which she never ceased to feel, she was exposed to perpetual suffering from the intrigues which

* Louis XIV. et son Siècle.

were set on foot on all sides to separate her from the King; which, combined with the harshness she continually experienced from *Madame*, kept her in a perpetual state of anxiety. Nevertheless, she bore all patiently, and forbore to utter a complaint, conscious, as she herself feelingly declares, that she was only paying the penalty of her faults. She was not, however, long fated to confine her grief to her own bosom; for, on one occasion, when it was her tour of duty about the person of the Princess, and that she was preparing to attend her to the funeral service of the Queen of Bohemia, then recently deceased, the Count of St. Aignan entered her apartment and delivered to her a note from the King, in which he requested her to return home immediately after the ceremony, as he had an affair of importance to communicate.

Naturally anxious to ascertain its nature, Mademoiselle de la Vallière questioned the messenger, who informed her that her enemies had just concerted a new plot, intended to ruin her in the King's affections; and that, on this occasion, they had involved the peace of the young Queen, by affecting to serve her in order to accomplish their purpose. He was about to be more explicit, when she was summoned to *Madame;* but she had heard enough to excite her uneasiness to a degree which she found it difficult to conceal. Nor did the expression of the King's countenance during the mass tend to remove her fears; he was pale, and occasionally looked fiercely round him, as though he sought some one upon whom he could wreak the anger by which he was evidently agitated; while, contrary to his usual rigid attention to the services of the Church, he addressed perpetual questions to the Marquis de Vardes, who knelt behind him.

It was, consequently, with increased alarm that La Vallière awaited his advent in her chamber on her return; but one glance convinced her that she at least had not incurred his displeasure, and he at once revealed to her the circumstance by which he was so deeply moved. A letter had been addressed to Maria Theresa, which was delivered to the Señora Molina, her Spanish waiting-woman, who, suspicious that it might contain something calculated to distress her Royal mistress, had forthwith carried it to the King. It was written in the Spanish language, but a translation had been appended which enabled the trembling Louise to read as follows :

" The King is involved in an intrigue of which your Majesty alone is ignorant. Mademoiselle de la Vallière is the object of this unworthy passion. This information is given to your Majesty by faithful servants. You must decide if you can love your husband in the arms of another, or if you will prevent a circumstance whose duration cannot tend to your honour."

While the unhappy La Vallière, drowned in tears, was endeavouring to conjecture from the hand of what new enemy this bolt had sped, the King himself, whose indignation increased every moment, informed her that it was a device of Madame de Navailles, and that nothing short of the ruin of herself and her husband would satisfy his vengeance for the affront which had been put upon them both ; nor was it without the most earnest entreaties that Mademoiselle de la Vallière could induce him to promise that he would limit their punishment to an immediate exile from the Capital.

It may be well to mention in this place that the unfortunate Duke and Duchess, who were deprived of their position at Court and banished, without a hope of future pardon, were totally guiltless of the letter which had excited the wrath of the King. The Countess of Soissons, hopeless of any change in the affection of Louis towards La Vallière, to whom she bore a mortal hatred, suddenly imagined that, could she succeed in acquainting Maria Theresa with the truth of a passion in which she had hitherto resolutely refused to place credence, her Spanish jealousy must inevitably cause a separation between the Monarch and his favourite; and in this belief she secured the envelope of a letter which the Queen had received from Madrid, and which she had thrown aside.

This done, she proceeded to the apartments of *Madame*, whom she requested to exert her influence in inducing the Count of Guiche to translate into Spanish for her a note of which she had brought a rough sketch in French. The Princess, who imagined that nothing more was intended than a jest to mystify some person about the Court, immediately sent for De Guiche, and having explained to him the service which Madame de Soissons required at his hands, left them while he accomplished his task. The Count had, however, no sooner run his eye over the paper which was placed in his hand than he indignantly refused to lend himself to so nefarious a proceeding; nor could all the blandishments of the Countess succeed in winning his compliance. The discussion lasted so long that

Madame returned to the room while it was at its height, and was immediately addressed by Madame de Soissons, who bade her place no further faith in the professions of the Duke of Guiche, as, after vowing himself to her interests, he had refused to further them by participating in a measure which would insure the dismission of La Vallière from the Court.

Suffice it that the arguments of the Princess, combined with those of her confidant, at length prevailed over the honour of the Count of Guiche, who affected, in order to serve his own passion for *Madame*, to become gradually convinced that, although the means employed were somewhat questionable, the motive was one of pure morality; there was, according to Madame de Soissons, an immoral connection to terminate—a husband to be restored to his wife, and a Queen to be saved from a life of sorrow; in short, a good action to be accomplished without difficulty, and, if carefully conducted, without danger.

While the Countess was speaking, *Madame* held in one hand the note which was to be translated, while, with a smile that she knew he would be unable to resist, she pointed to a writing-stand beside her, and then motioned to the Count to seat himself. He obeyed, but with a compunction which still made him hesitate, until the Princess, motioning to Madame de Soissons and the Marquis de Vardes to leave the room, commenced dictating the sentences he was to translate, with another sunny smile, which he answered by exclaiming,

" Be it so, then, since it is your will; fortunately it involves my life, should it ever be discovered, for nothing save the scaffold will expiate such a crime. But it is your pleasure; and for your sake I am ready to become an anonymous assassin—to lose my self-respect—to write this letter."

Unhappily, the Princess, strong in her aversion to Mademoiselle de la Vallière, and confident in the good management of the Countess, considered all discovery impossible; and thus the letter was translated with a careful imitation of the writing of the Queen of Spain; and it was no sooner finished than the Countess hastened to inclose it in its cover, well aware that if she suffered it to remain in the hands of the Count of Guiche, a return of better feeling would induce him to destroy it. M. de Vardes undertook its transmission to the Louvre, through a courier who was about to quit his service; and the Count saw it carried away with a pang of remorse, which not even the gracious acknowledgments of *Madame* had power to overcome.

As we have already stated, the letter was delivered to the Señora Molina, who, well acquainted with the autograph of the Queen of Spain, and discovering in the address certain indications of an imperfect attempt at its imitation, immediately conceived the idea that it was some anonymous communication calculated to wound her mistress; and believing that with such a suspicion she ran no risk by confiding in the Queen-mother, she immediately carried it to Anne of Austria, who, delighted to have an opportunity of giving this additional proof to her son of the public indignation excited by his attachment for Mademoiselle de la Vallière, desired Molina to deliver the letter to the King.

The waiting-woman seized the opportunity of his leaving the council-chamber to approach Louis with the open letter in her hand, and to inform him, that by a providential inspiration, fearing it might contain intelligence of the death of the King of Spain, who had long been dangerously indisposed, she had unsealed the packet before giving it to the Queen.

Louis unfolded the paper, and the blood rushed to his brow as he perused its contents; and then, after compelling the bearer to pledge her oath that she had not communicated its contents to her Royal mistress, he hastened to the apartments of Madame de Soissons, believing that her sagacity would enable her to discover the delinquent. It is needless, however, to state that, although the Countess was not backward in pointing his suspicions in more than one direction, she afforded him no clew to the actual culprit; and it was reserved to M. de Vardes, when questioned in his turn by the Monarch, to centre them upon the unhappy Duchess of Navailles, who paid the penalty of his treachery during three weary years.

Shortly after this event Mademoiselle de la Vallière became the mother of a son, who lived but ten months, and whose existence, from the caution of those about her, was known only to a few persons. Immediately after its birth, the King expressed a wish that while she retained her post at the court of *Madame*, she should cease to fulfil its functions; but to this La Vallière objected, upon the ground that such an arrangement was without precedent, and would only increase the virulence of her enemies; and as Louis was silenced, if not convinced by the argument, she was comparatively surprised when, on presenting herself as usual at the toilet of *Madame,* her Royal Highness informed her that thenceforward she would dispense with her official services, which under present circumstances no longer became her, adding that she did so by command of the King.

The extreme harshness with which this favour was accorded rendered it eminently painful to the erring maid of honour, who was crushed beneath the weight of her conscience, and found her only consolation in the conviction that she was indebted for the scorn and coldness of the Princess rather to the jealousy with which she regarded a rival than to her horror of the crime she affected to condemn. Nevertheless, this constant recurrence of mortification preyed upon the mind of Mademoiselle de la Vallière; and, combined with her separation from her child, affected both her health and spirits to a degree which not even the augmented tenderness of the King had power to remove.

During the carnival of 1663, the Crown Prince of Denmark, who was making the tour of Europe, arrived in Paris, where he was welcomed with great distinction; and MADEMOISELLE, who had been exiled to her estate of St. Fargeau, for having refused to marry the King of Portugal, received constant letters from the Court, in which her correspondents expatiated on the fine person of the Prince, his exquisite dancing, and the perfection with which he spoke the French language, coupled with assurances that he aspired to her hand; and that, having expressed to the King a desire to wait upon her in her exile, his Majesty had readily given his consent to the visit.

MADEMOISELLE was, however, just then in the vein of opposition, and declared her resolution to decline the proffered honour; alleging, as an excuse, that her house was not yet in a state which would enable her to receive guests of his quality. Her mood was, moreover, rendered still less complying by the fact that she had endeavoured to temporise with the King, by offering thus tardily to accept the hand of the Duke of Savoy, which had been proposed to her; but Louis rejected the compromise, telling her, in a bitter manner, that he should marry her as might best serve his own interests; and during her banishment, this very Duke of Savoy, whose gallant bearing and personal advantages had produced their effect even upon her haughty nature, during his apparition at Lyons with the Princess Marguerite, had become the husband of her sister, Mademoiselle de Valois, whose reception at the Court of Turin had been most brilliant.

It is probable, however, that MADEMOISELLE afterwards repented her abruptness; and finding that the pleasures of the Court were preferable to the monotonous occupation of building and furnishing, with which she had endeavoured to beguile her banishment, became anxious to quit her solitude; for she, ere long, wrote to the King to state that, having caused a swamp upon her estate to be drained, the air had become so overcharged with miasma that her health was giving way; and she was shortly afterwards recalled.

Soon after her return to Paris,* there was a grand gala at Court, on Twelfth-night; when, either by

* Jour des Rois.

chance or design, the Prince of Denmark drew the bean,* and immediately selected MADEMOISELLE as the companion of his transitory honours: a circumstance which gave evident satisfaction to the King, who had already privately offered the hand of his cousin to the young heir of Denmark, affecting to be urged to this measure by political considerations, but probably anxious to rid himself of the continual annoyances to which he was subjected by her overweening pretensions and perpetual discontent.

MADEMOISELLE, however, rejected this new prospect of a throne as decidedly as she had refused that by which it had been preceded, even declining to adduce any reason for her decision; and thus again incurred the King's displeasure immediately after her restoration to favour so greatly, that he did not scruple to remark that he could not in any way account for her conduct, save by the supposition that she still preserved a hope of becoming Queen of France, as she refused all the Princes who were proposed to her; in which case, he added, that she was only injuring herself, for that should it please God to spare him longer than the Queen, it was assuredly not Mademoiselle de Montpensier who would afterwards share his throne.

Were any further proof requisite of the extreme depravity of the French Court at that period, it would be supplied by the fact that the King, undeterred by the

---

* The ceremony of "drawing characters" in France is different from our own. A single bean is mixed with the ingredients of the cake, and the person in whose portion it is discovered becomes King or Queen for the evening, and chooses a consort; and both are afterwards attended, by the rest of the company, with all the ceremonial due to their temporary rank.

increasing devotion and piety of his Royal mother, who now passed the greater portion of her time in the convent of Val-de-Grâce, importuned her to receive Mademoiselle de la Vallière, even at a time when she was scarcely visible to the most attached of her friends ; nor could the undisguised repugnance which she evinced to profane the holy retreat, where she sought to forget all worldly passions and worldly animosities, induce the infatuated Monarch to withdraw his request.

Deeply attached to Maria Theresa, to whose forbearance and uncomplaining patience she was no stranger, she naturally shrunk from all contact with a person by whom she had been so deeply wronged; and the many amiable qualities of the erring woman whom she was required to welcome, in order to assure to her a position in society to which she was entitled neither by her birth nor her conduct, could not blind her to the extent and mischievous nature of her fault. But Louis was resolute; and surely the devoted and deceived Mary de Mancini was revenged, when at length a Royal carriage drove into the courtyard of the pious nuns of Val-de-Grâce, and that the son of Anne of Austria ascended the stairs, entered her oratory—that sanctuary which should have been her refuge from the profligacy and vices of a Court—and presenting his mistress, said, with a calm smile upon his lips, " *Mother*, here is Mademoiselle de la Vallière, whom you have condescended to send for."

The soul-stricken Magdalen, as she looked on the stern brow and cold eye of the coerced and indignant Queen, would have knelt ; and even when the hand of her Royal mistress raised her from the floor to a low stool beside her own seat, she could not, during the brief interview, sufficiently control her feeling of humiliation to remember any portion of the conversation. With the King she could be, and she was to the last, only a loving and devoted woman, who had sacrificed all, even her self-esteem, to a passion too mighty for resistance; but in the presence of his injured and dying mother she forgot her love in her remorse.

The affection of the King for Mademoiselle de la Vallière being now recognised, the cessation of mystery caused an equal cessation of interest on the subject, save as regarded those who were affected by its existence; but it was far otherwise with the passion of the Count of Guiche for *Madame;* and accordingly, after the birth of her daughter, Maria Louisa d'Orleans, it once more became a general topic of conversation at Court, and so extremely displeased the Monarch that he desired the Marquis de Vardes to inform him of all he knew on the subject.

De Vardes, who feared that the imprudence of the Count would, ere long, betray his secret, and who was, consequently, anxious to remove him from the Court while there was yet time, did not affect to deny the truth, although he endeavoured to palliate his fault; but the anger of the King, who lost sight of his own errors while condemning those of others, was so vehement, that the Marquis endeavoured to calm him by applauding his expressed determination to separate De Guiche from the object of his passion—only suggesting that the interest of both *Monsieur* and *Madame* exacted that his dismissal should not carry with it the appearance of disgrace, and hinting that it would be politic to give to the imprudent courtier the command of the troops at Nancy, which would impart to his exile the air of a signal favour.

Louis XIV., delighted by a measure which would at the same time terminate the romantic attachment of the Count, and gratify his father, the Marshal of Grammont, instantly acted upon this advice; and De Guiche departed for Lorraine with despair in his heart, after having been compelled to receive the congratulations of half the Court.

CHAPTER VII

ABOUT this time, intelligence reached the Capital
of the death of the Duke of Longueville at his
government of Normandy, and of another actor in the
Fronde in the person of the Marshal of la Meilleraye,
whose son had become Duke of Mazarin by his
marriage with Hortensia de Mancini. But what was
still more calculated to shed a veil of mourning over
the festivities which had hitherto succeeded each other
in rapid succession, was the fact that the illness of the

Queen-mother increased so rapidly as to excite the fears of all around her.

Anne of Austria had enjoyed the rare privilege, so seldom accorded to her sex, of growing old without in any very eminent degree losing her personal advantages. Her hands and arms, which had always been singularly beautiful, remained smooth and round, and delicately white; not a wrinkle marred the dignity of her noble forehead; and her eyes, which were remarkably fine, lost neither their brightness nor their expression; and yet for years she had been suffering physical pangs, only the more poignant from the resolution with which she concealed them. Compelled at last to confide in the faculty, she had in vain applied in succession every remedy which had been suggested to her, and at length the disease made such inroad upon her constitution that her strength began visibly to give way. The summer sojourn of the King at Versailles, in 1664, was consequently abandoned, while the young Queen was so painfully affected by the state of her Royal mother-in-law, to whom she was tenderly attached, that her health gave way beneath the shock, and she was so violently attacked by measles that her life was endangered.

On this occasion all the better feelings of the King were awakened; and regardless of the expostulations of those about him, he could not be induced to leave her bedside, where he remained day and night till he became infected with the complaint, and for the first four days was not expected to survive. On the fifth, however, the disease weakened, and he was removed to St. Cloud, where *Madame* was then residing, and where he was consequently under the same roof with Mademoiselle de la Vallière.

During his sojourn in that palace, the *legate à latere* arrived to make the *amende honourable*, which had been demanded by Louis XIV. for the insult offered to his Ambassador at Rome, and was received by the King in his bedchamber, within the balustrade, where, as a signal honour, he was permitted to seat himself.* All the principal nobles of the Court were present, and heard, with natural exultation, from the document read by the Cardinal, that the Pope, recognising the justice of the displeasure of the French Monarch, consented to disband the Corsican guard, and to raise within the walls of Rome a pyramid commemorative of the insult and its reparation.

The Cardinal Chigi was the first Legate ever despatched by the Roman Court to sue for the pardon of a European Sovereign; their province had hitherto invariably been to give laws and to impose tithes. But on this occasion Louis XIV., not satisfied by so temporary a manifestation of repentance on the part of his Holiness as the disbanding of a regiment of guards, and the erection of a monument which might readily be removed, or which must in any event disappear in the lapse of time, insisted on the restoration of Castro and Conciglione to the Duke of Parma, and that the Duke of Modena should receive a compensation for his claims on Comachio; thus making an insult to his Ambassador subservient to investing himself with the solid advantage of standing forth as the protector of the Italian Princes.†

---

* Versailles Ancien et Moderne.   † Le Siècle de Louis XIV.

The treaty of reconciliation was no sooner concluded than Louis XIV. gave a series of *fêtes*, in
honour, as he publicly asserted, of his distinguished
guest, but which he privately dedicated to La Vallière.
Races at the ring, concerts on the water, balls and
banquets, succeeded each other with a rapidity and
splendour which dazzled and delighted the Roman
envoy; while, on his side, that dignitary rendered himself extremely popular with the whole Court—an
effect the more easily produced from the fact of his
being a handsome man, not more than thirty years of
age, tall in stature, with finely-arched black eyebrows,
hands which became the envy of half the ladies of the
Royal circle, and an air of dignified suavity that
savoured more of the courtier than the churchman.

Notwithstanding the pleasure which he evidently
derived from the amusements into which he so readily
entered, his hosts were nevertheless somewhat startled
on witnessing the relish with which he assisted at the
performance of the *Princesse d'Elide*, and still more
so by his request, on its conclusion, that the author
might be presented to him; when the Prince de Conti
lost no time in introducing Molière, who was overwhelmed with praise by the Legate, and with assurances that he had never seen any farce by which he
had been so much diverted.

The admiration of the Cardinal was very gratifying
to Louis XIV., who regarded the great dramatist as one
of the most distinguished men in his kingdom, and
who had, on perceiving Molière (who in his official
capacity of court upholsterer was, in conjunction with
his colleague, Delobel, engaged in arranging the

tapestries of the orchestra), on an occasion when he was about to take his frugal breakfast of bread and weak wine and water, desired his attendants to bring forward a folding stool, and made the dramatist take a seat by his side, in order to ımpress upon those about him, who affected to despise the plebeian genius, the estimation in which he was held by their Monarch.

The greater portion of the summer of 1663 had been passed amid these perpetual festivities, when, in the month of August, France was again threatened with a war, which was, however, averted by the weakness of her adversary. It may be remembered that the Duke of Lorraine had signed a treaty by which he bequeathed his principality to France after his death, on condition that the King would allow him to raise a million of revenue during his life; and that the Princes of the Blood of Lorraine should be recognised as Princes of the Blood of France; while, on his side, Louis XIV. had exacted that one of the frontier fortresses of the principality should be forthwith surrendered to the French. The unfortunate Charles IV., a brave soldier, but a feeble, vacillating, and imprudent Prince, although he had authorised the verification of this treaty by the Parliament, after a thousand subterfuges and delays, had at length refused to fulfil his compact, and it was decided that he should at once be compelled to do so.

Meanwhile, the Count of Guiche—whose honourable exile was embittered by constant letters from the Marquis de Vardes, who, during his absence, was endeavouring to supplant his friend in the affections of the Duchess of Orleans, whose smiles were also sought

by the Prince de Marsillac and the Chevalier de Lorraine, to both of whom she was utterly indifferent, and
who, in order to conceal his own turpitude, hinted at
her marked preference of the Prince—became highly
incensed, and wrote reproachfully to *Madame*, who, in
her indignation, complained to M. de Vardes of the
presumption of her old favourite.

This was precisely the point at which the Marquis
had aimed, and, far from endeavouring to defend his
friend, he immediately seized the opportunity of alarm-
ing the fears of the Princess, by representing the
danger to which she was exposed from the jealousy of
the Count, and the necessity there existed for the
restoration of her letters; which, however inconsequent they might really be, would, in the event of
their becoming suspected, be assuredly misinterpreted,
and thus injure both parties. In the first burst of her
displeasure, *Madame* acted upon this insidious advice;
and De Guiche, revolted by a want of confidence
which impugned his honour, did not attempt to re-
monstrate, but at once confided to the Marquis the
casket which contained the correspondence.

This was no sooner in the possession of the Princess
than she repented her precipitancy, for she felt the
wound which her implied suspicion must have inflicted
upon a high-minded man, whose only error had been
his headlong and uncalculating passion for herself; but
it was too late to regret the step when she held in her
hands the letters she had reclaimed, and learned that
the Count of Guiche had fallen dangerously ill at
Nancy.

The latter intelligence had no sooner reached the

Countess of Guiche than she resolved to join her husband, in order to solace his sickness by her attentions; and the heart-stricken invalid could not remain insensible to such a sacrifice, although he had never affected any attachment towards a wife who had been forced upon him by his family.* He consequently exerted himself to render her sojourn with the army less monotonous than she must have been prepared to find it; and all Paris ere long learned that the Countess was surrounded by gayety, and the object of her husband's unceasing devotion.

No one experienced more gratification from this intelligence than the King, who had lately purchased Dunkirk from the English, and was preparing to seize Marsal from the Duke of Lorraine; and in his satisfaction at so happy a change in his old playfellow, he caused it to be announced to him that he was about to arrive in person at Nancy to superintend the siege, accompanied by *Monsieur*. The Count was careful to profit by so admirable an opportunity of recovering the good graces of the Monarch; and, aware of his taste for display and ceremony, he accordingly lost no time in preparing for him a triumphal entry into the city, which so much gratified Louis that no shade of displeasure remained towards M. de Guiche, who suddenly found himself once more on the very pinnacle of Court favour.

Notwithstanding this extreme graciousness, however, the King retained considerable curiosity to learn all the details of the intimacy which had existed be-

* Mademoiselle de Béthune, Countess of Guiche, was the daughter of the Duke of Sully, and granddaughter of the Chancellor Seguier.

tween *Madame* and his host; and in order to accomplish this, he affected in their private interviews to know far more than he was in reality aware of, and mentioned the secret meetings of the Count and the Princess as matters with which he was so well acquainted that it was needless for De Guiche to deny them.

Duped by this apparent candour, and glad, in all probability to be enabled to convince his Royal master of his frankness without betraying the confidence which had been reposed in him by the Princess, the Count related every circumstance which had occurred, insisting throughout that nothing had taken place which could in any way affect the honour of her Royal Highness. Had Louis XIV. been discreet no evil consequences could have arisen from this revelation, even extorted as it was by the subtile inferences of the King himself; but, unfortunately, it afforded so favourable an opportunity of intimidating *Madame*, that he was unable to deny himself the gratification of informing her that he was master of her secret; and she was the more enraged by the discovery from the fact that, after the departure of Louis for Lorraine, she had written to M. de Guiche to warn him, if he valued her friendship, not to suffer the King to prevail on him to make the slightest disclosures.

Before her letter arrived at Nancy, however, there remained no more to tell; and on the return of the Monarch to Paris, he had no sooner proved that he was aware of all the detail of the intrigue than she addressed a letter to the Count, in which she commanded him never to appear in her presence, or to utter her name, under pain of her lasting hatred. In vain did he write, again and again, explaining all the circumstances under which he had been betrayed; his letters were returned unanswered; and at length, despairing that he should ever be able to justify himself in her eyes, he requested permission of the King to serve in the Polish army—a measure to which Louis was at first opposed, but which he ultimately conceded, on learning how much he had himself been instrumental in its adoption.

The taking of Marsal, where he had fought bravely, permitting M. de Guiche to resign with honour the command which he held in Lorraine, he embarked for Dantzic, careless of the fate which might await him. The Monarch was, however, sufficiently generous to reassure *Madame*, after his departure, on the nature of the confidence which he had extorted from the self-exiled Count; and when she learned that, far from having boasted of her favour, he had convinced the King that her sole error had been that of permitting him to love her, the Princess thought only of the means of recompensing him for all the suffering which he had undergone on her account; and ere long she despatched her miniature by a trusty messenger, who transmitted it to the Count in Poland, where, a short time afterwards, it saved his life in battle, a ball having struck the case in which it was contained suspended by a chain about his neck.*

The continued victories of the King of Poland began, however, after a time, to make Louis regret

* Histoire de Madame Henriette d'Angleterre, par la Comtesse de la Fayette.

the assent which he had given to the request of the
Count of Guiche to serve in his army; and the annoyance that he felt whenever he encountered the name
of one of his best officers, in the despatches which
reached him filled with details of the engagements
gained over the Muscovites, despite all the glory which
accrued to the name of France from the gallantry of
the Count, induced him to determine on his return;
and he accordingly desired the Marshal of Grammont
to recall him in his name.   The letter of the Marshal
reached M. de Guiche on his return from Varsovie,
while John Casimir was arranging a peace with the
insurgents of the Ukraine, and an armistice with the
Turks; and scarcely allowing himself time to take
leave of the King, and to communicate to him the
order which he had received from his own Sovereign
to return home, he commenced his journey the same
night, and arrived in Paris, exhausted with fatigue and
wild with joy.

Monsieur, when he first saw him in the circle of the
King, bowed gravely without uttering a syllable of
welcome; *Madame* affected an indifference which she
was far from feeling; and the Marquis de Vardes, conscious that by his treachery he must have converted a
friend into an enemy, met him with an elaborate po-
liteness which was as elaborately returned.

The position of each party was embarrassing, but it
soon became more so; for the Chevalier de Lorraine,
piqued by the coldness of the Princess, affected extreme devotion to several ladies of the Court; and his
universal homage created such amusement, that he
was tormented by all his friends to confess who was

the real object of his preference. Thus urged he mentioned Mademoiselle de Fiennes, one of the maids of honour of *Madame*, when the Marquis de Vardes, who was present, and who had his own subject of annoyance, asked him superciliously why he did not rather address his vows to her mistress.

The Count of Guiche overheard the inquiry; but from respect to the Queen, in whose circle the conversation had taken place, he made no rejoinder until the next morning, when he sent a challenge to De Vardes. The King was, however, immediately informed of the circumstance, and forbade the meeting; while *Madame*, to whom it had also been confided, hastened to complain of the indignity to his Majesty, who sent the Marquis to the Bastille. In her anger the Princess did not spare the Countess of Soissons, to whose influence she attributed the insult; and among other remarks which she addressed to the King, she said that she was not surprised to find herself the victim of the Superintendent's malice, when those who were most dear to his Majesty could not escape; and upon an inquiry of her meaning, she informed him that on one occasion, when Madame de la Vallière had taken precedence of the wife of a President, the Countess had remarked to the Duchess of Ventadour, that she was aware that La Vallière was lame, but she never before knew that she was blind.

The anger of the King was unbounded, and he immediately ordered that the Countess of Soissons should be banished from the Court; while the astonishment and fury of the Superintendent were beyond bounds when the order was conveyed to her. She uttered in-

vectives against the Sovereign, who had, she said,
sacrificed her to a nobody; against the two Queens,
who ought to intercede for her; but especially against
Madame, upon whom she declared that she would
soon have ample revenge. She kept her word, but in
a manner which, although it was eminently mortifying
to the Princess, proved far more fatal to herself; for it
was possible that the King would after a time have
forgiven her offence, had she not, in her weak desire
for revenge, after accusing alike friends and enemies
of crimes which in all probability were the offspring
of her own malice, ended by relating to Louis the
whole history of the Spanish letter, although in a
manner which exculpated both herself and M. de
Vardes, and cast all the stigma upon *Madame* and the
Count of Guiche.

The King, more and more exasperated by what he
heard, instantly summoned the Princess; who, on being confronted with the Countess of Soissons, related
the whole plot, even to its minutest details, and so
thoroughly laid it open that Louis became convinced
of her sincerity; and on ascertaining that the original
draft of the letter was in the handwriting of M. de
Vardes, ordered his immediate transfer to the Fortress
of Pignerolle, declaring to Madame de Soissons that
if he could conceive any punishment more heavy than
that which he had inflicted on herself he would condemn her to its endurance.

Madame, who felt that neither herself nor the Count
of Guiche had been quite blameless in the affair, obtained a promise that her accomplice should not be in
any way subjected to the Royal displeasure; but on

the intelligence of M. de Vardes's arrest, the Marshal of Grammont became alarmed, and sent his son to Holland, although he was at the time labouring under a severe indisposition.

This event divided the whole Court into two distinct parties. The Queen-mother headed that of the Superintendent; but her interest was powerless against the will of the King. Maria Theresa refused to interfere in any way; while *Monsieur* could not conceal his delight at this third exile of the Count of Guiche. With the exception of a few of the younger nobility, who missed the brilliant saloon of Madame de Soissons, and the immediate friends of Anne of Austria, who, as a matter of course, regulated their feelings by hers, little regret was, however, really experienced at the banishment of the haughty and sarcastic Countess; the greatest commiseration was bestowed upon M. de Vardes, who was, nevertheless, the greatest culprit of all, but no one dared openly to espouse his cause; and in a Court constituted like that which we are endeavouring to describe, he was ere long forgotten. The Duke of Mazarin was the only individual who ventured to lift up his voice against the sentence of the King; for, although he had no great affection for his sister-in-law, the eccentricity of his character always induced him to act differently from those about him, and in this instance it prompted a proceeding so extraordinary, that it became the subject of universal comment.

Having waited upon the Monarch at his *lever*, he approached him with an air of profound mystery, and said, solemnly, " Sire, Ste. Genevieve appeared to me last night. She is much offended by the conduct of your Majesty, and has foretold to me that if you do not reform your morals the greatest misfortunes will fall upon your kingdom."

The whole circle stood aghast; but the King, without exhibiting the slightest emotion, replied slowly and sternly, " And I, Monsieur de Mazarin, have recently had several visions, by which I have been warned that the late Cardinal, your uncle, plundered my people, and that it is time to make his heirs disgorge the booty. Remember this, and be persuaded that the very next time you permit yourself to offer to me unsolicited advice I shall act upon the mysterious information I have received."

The Duke attempted no reply, and shortly afterwards left the apartment, much disappointed at the ill success of his stratagem.*

* Mémoires de Madame de Vallière.

CHAPTER VIII

Decline of Anne of Austria—Recovery of the Young Queen—
A Courtier's Compliment—Susceptibility of the Queen-mother
—Death of Philip IV. of Spain—Projects of Louis XIV.—
Sufferings of Anne of Austria—Renewed Festivities at Court
—The Royal Deathbed—Ill-timed Etiquette—The Holy Oils—
Death of Anne of Austria—Condescension of Mademoiselle—
The Archbishop and the Queen's Heart—The Royal Funeral
at St. Denis—Birth of Mademoiselle de Blois—La Vallière
Created a Duchess—Legitimation of La Vallière's Children—
Birth of Louis de Bourbon—Madame Colbert Governess to
Mademoiselle de Blois and the Count of Vermandois—Rec-
onciliation of La Vallière with Her Mother—Distaste of Louis
XIV. for Madame de St. Rémy—Decline of the King's Pas-
sion for La Vallière—A New Favourite.

MEANWHILE, the Queen-mother rapidly declined, and the regular faculty having failed to
stay the progress of the evil, she placed herself in the
hands of empirics, by whom it was aggravated; while
Maria Theresa gradually recovered her health, and was
enabled once more to devote all her care and attention
to her suffering relative. Vallot, the King's physician,
and Seguin, who was the medical attendant of Anne
of Austria, could not agree upon the system to be
pursued; and while the invalid was in suspense as to
their final decision, the insidious disease made rapid

at the convent of Val-de-Grâce, of which she had for
several years been a frequent inmate, she felt convinced
that, beyond all doubt, the evil had become incurable;
and although, during the last twelve or fifteen years,
she had seen many cases of the same kind among the
nuns (by which she had been so terrified as to make
it her daily prayer to God that she might be spared so
bitter a trial as theirs), she nevertheless no sooner ascertained the nature of her affliction, than she summoned all her fortitude to support it; and frequently
expressed a trust that she should be enabled by means
of her physical sufferings to expiate her sins.

Ere long she was perfectly aware of her danger;
but even had she sought to deceive herself as to its
extent, the want of caution observed by those who
approached her would have rendered such a delusion
impossible. As an example of this extraordinary and
ill-timed frankness, on one occasion, when she had suffered more than usual and was greatly exhausted, her
immediate end being anticipated, M. de Beringhen,
the first valet-de-chambre, who was one of the oldest
and most faithful of her attendants, was admitted to
her bedside, and on seeing him she exclaimed, " Ah!
monsieur, we must part!"   To which the Court serv-
itor coolly replied, " Madam, you will readily understand with what grief your servants receive such an
assurance; but it must be a consolation to them as
well as to yourself to feel that by dying at once your
Majesty will escape great torment and great inconvenience, inasmuch as the disease under which you
labour becomes after a time very noisome." *

* Anne of Austria died of cancer.

The afflicted Queen made no reply, but turned upon the pillow as if to avoid all further sight of so awkward a consoler; and the congratulation which he had attempted to couple with his condolence was the more inconsiderate, as the unfortunate Queen, despite the prediction of her medical attendants, was still fated to linger several months before she was released from her bitter trial.

The sufferings of the unhappy Anne of Austria must indeed have been extreme, when, superadded to the physical agony of which she was so long the victim, her peculiar fastidiousness of scent and touch are remembered. Throughout the whole of her illness she had adopted every measure to conceal even from herself the effects of her infirmity. She constantly held in her hand a large fan of Spanish leather, and saturated her linen with the most powerful perfumes; while her sense of contact was so acute and so irritable that it was with the utmost difficulty cambric could be procured sufficiently fine for her use; and upon one occasion, when Cardinal Mazarin was jesting with her upon this defect, he told her that " if she were damned, her eternal punishment would be sleeping in linen sheets." *

Immediately that the danger of the Queen-mother became imminent, *Monsieur* hastened to her bedside; and it was only some hours afterwards that she was visited by the King, who did not suffer private feeling to interfere with public business, even in the case of a dying parent, and whose tardy visit might have been indefinitely postponed could he have foreseen that the

* Louis XIV., sa Cour, et le Regent.

agony upon which he compelled himself for a short time to look was incident only upon a crisis of the complaint; for partial convalescence enabled the unhappy sufferer to support the melancholy tidings which soon afterwards reached her of the death of her brother, Philip IV. of Spain.

This intelligence produced very varied effects upon the different members of the Royal family. The young Queen was overwhelmed with grief, and mourned for her father with unaffected sorrow. Anne of Austria shed but few tears, for she felt that she should soon join him in the tomb; while Louis XIV. looked upon the event as a Sovereign rather than a kinsman, and saw at once the benefit which might accrue to himself from the event ; and it is probable that from that very moment he meditated the succession to the Spanish Crown.

Philip IV. had become, by his first wife (the sister of Louis XIII.), the father of the Princess Maria Theresa, now married to her cousin, Louis XIV.; a marriage by which the Spanish Monarchy had at length fallen into the house of Bourbon, so long its enemy. By his second marriage, with Mary-Anne of Austria, he had issue, Charles II., the heir to the throne —a weak and sickly child, and sole survivor of three sons, two of whom had died in their infancy. It is true that, at the period of his alliance with Maria Theresa, the French King had, in his marriage treaty, agreed to resign every claim to all and any of the kingdom of Spain; but he instantly remembered that on the other hand that treaty had been already violated, inasmuch as the five hundred thousand crowns which

were the dower of his wife had never been paid;
nor did he care to call to mind that the dower of the
daughter of Henry IV. had also been merely nominal.
And, under these circumstances, he decided that
Flanders and Franche-Comté must, according to the
jurisprudence of those provinces, return to his wife,
notwithstanding her renunciation. He accordingly
caused his right to be investigated by his own Council, who declared it to be incontestible; but the
Council and the confessor of the widow of Philip
IV. decided precisely the reverse; and the Spanish
Queen had in her favour one powerful argument
in the law laid down by Charles V., had the laws
of Charles V. been acknowledged by the French
Court.*

Meanwhile the Queen-mother was lingering on, a
prey to the greatest physical agony, and had become
so much exhausted by her long-continued suffering as
to faint when she was removed from one bed to another. But when the winter brought its habitual train
of festivities, as she still survived, the Court gradually
resumed its accustomed habits; for she had been so
long an invalid that those about her had become in-
ured to the sight of her suffering.

On the 5th of January *Monsieur* gave a ball, at
which the King appeared in a suit of violet-coloured
velvet, as mourning for his Royal father-in-law, so covered, however, with pearls and diamonds that the
colour of the material could not be distinguished;
and on the following day the unfortunate Anne of
Austria became so much worse, that a stop was put to

* Le Siècle de Louis XIV. *Francheville.*

all amusements.   Her illness increased during the
night, and although in the morning she slept for an
hour or two, the disease made such rapid progress that
it was evident her end was fast approaching; and she
accordingly began to prepare for death, and received
with great and Christian fortitude the assurance of her
physician that she had only a few hours to live.   She
then asked for her confessor and requested every one
to retire, declaring that she wanted nothing, and could
think only of God.

The King, the Queen, *Monsieur, Madame*, and
MADEMOISELLE, accordingly passed into her cabinet,
while an express was despatched for the sacrament;
and when there, says the latter, with supreme self-
possession, "in order not to remain useless, we
settled the ceremonials of the mourning, and spoke of
other matters which required arrangement, and the
division of the apartments at St. Germain, determining
that the King should leave for Versailles the moment
that she should be no more; that *Monsieur* should go
to St. Cloud; and that I should remain to order what
was necessary.   The King himself commanded the
carriages."*

When the approach of the Archbishop of Auch,
attended by the other almoners, with the Holy Viaticum was announced, a discussion arose among the
illustrious party in the cabinet with regard to the ceremonial which should be observed, and an appeal was
made to Madame de Motteville, who replied that in
the case of the late King the Princes had advanced as
far as the outer door of the palace to receive the pro-

* Mémoires de Mademoiselle de Montpensier.

cession, and that she thought it would be wise to act upon that precedent.

MADEMOISELLE, however, objected with considerable haughtiness to so extreme a measure, declaring that she could not consent to establish any custom of the kind; and that as it was her privilege to walk first, she should not advance beyond the middle of the Court of the Louvre, which she considered quite sufficient for the holy pyx, as no more could be done for the sacrament itself. Her decision was admitted; and the Royal party consequently proceeded no further than the distance she had named.*

When about to receive the extreme unction, as the priests were preparing to anoint her ears with the holy oils, the dying Queen desired Madame de Flex, her lady of honour, to be careful to raise the borders of her cap, lest the oil should touch them and give them an unpleasant smell; and the ceremony was no sooner at an end than the King fainted, and was carried into an adjoining apartment, where he was with difficulty restored to consciousness. Finally, at six o'clock on the following morning, she expired, and Madame de Flex carried her keys to the King; her will was then brought from the cabinet, and read before the whole of the Royal family save *Monsieur*, who refused to remain; and M. le Tellier had no sooner completed the reading than the King got into his carriage and departed.†

When the funeral equipage arrived which was to convey the heart of the deceased Queen to the convent

---

* Mémoires de Madame de Montespan.
† Mémoires de Mademoiselle de Montpensier.

of Val-de-Grâce, to which she had bequeathed it,
MADEMOISELLE, in a mourning cloak, attended by
Madame de Longueville and the Princess of Carignan,
met the Archbishop of Auch at the foot of the grand
staircase, and desired him to deposit the heart in the
seat of honour, and to place himself beside it, declaring that on this occasion she would yield to him the
privilege of her rank; and upon some hesitation on
the part of the prelate, she added, with more frankness
than civility, " I shall prefer placing myself on the back
seat, on account of the disease of which she died."

This reasoning was unanswerable; and the Archbishop accordingly shared the cushion which bore the
senseless relic of the once powerful Queen-Regent of
France.*

On the following evening,† at seven o'clock, the
body of the Queen-mother left the Louvre, and arrived at St. Denis at eleven, where the mourners were
detained an hour and a half in the church, listening to
the harangue pronounced by the Archbishop of Auch
at the portal on delivering up the body, and the reply
of the prior; after which the funeral obsequies were
performed, and only brought to a conclusion at two
o'clock in the morning—a similar service having taken
place simultaneously at Nôtre-Dame—and this ceremony over, the Court returned to Paris.

In the following October, Mademoiselle de la Val-
liere became the mother of a daughter,‡ and about six

---

* Mémoires de Madame de Montespan.
† 21st January, 1666.
‡ Anna Maria of Bourbon, afterwards legitimatised, who married,
in 1680, Louis Armand de Bourbon, Prince de Conti.

months subsequent to that event, despite her earnest solicitations that he would permit her to remain in her partial obscurity, Louis XIV. formally conferred upon his mistress the estate of Vaujours and the barony of St. Christophe, which he had caused to be erected into a duchy-peerage; and legitimatised her child, by an act passed at St. Germain-en-Laye at the commencement of May, 1667, and registered by the Parliament in the same month.

On the second of December, in the following year, Mademoiselle (or, as she was now called, Madame) de la Vallière gave birth to a third child, a son—who was legitimatised, like his sister, under the name of Louis de Bourbon—and was afterwards known as the Count of Vermandois.

Thenceforward all privacy was impossible. M. Colbert, who owed everything to the King, intrusted the education of the (now) Royal children to his wife, by whom they were brought up under his own eye. The elder, who took the name of Mademoiselle de Blois, was of surpassing beauty, and the gradual decrease of the King's passion for their mother never for an instant induced any diminution of tenderness towards her children, whom he idolised.

At this period the Marquise de St. Rémy, upon the representations of the Dowager-Duchess of Orleans, consented to see her daughter, whose lapse from virtue she had hitherto resented so much as to have altogether withdrawn her countenance from her in consequence; but she did so with a coldness that convinced her erring child she had obeyed the wishes of her Royal mistress rather than the impulse of her own will; and

the King never forgave her this demonstration of her
feelings.   In vain did La Vallière endeavour to make
him comprehend that to a parent the reputation of her
daughter must be dearer than anything on earth.
Louis XIV., strong in his egotism, would not understand that his love could be otherwise than an honour
to all who might become involved in its effects; and
thus he was with difficulty induced to tolerate the
marchioness, and never evinced towards her a single
mark of favour.

This fact alone might have convinced the unhappy
Duchess that her power over the affections of her
Royal lover was actually, even if not ostensibly, di-
minishing.   Some months previously he would have
listened to her arguments and yielded to her reasons;
but now, although she had acquired as a mother a
more feasible claim upon his heart, she had begun to
fade beneath anxiety and care; as her bloom had been
her greatest attraction, she was no longer so well able
to compete with the younger and happier beauties by
whom she was surrounded; nor was so supreme an
egotist as Louis XIV. likely to remain long blind to
such a fact; while it is certain that one of the handsomest women of the Court not only perceived but
resolved to profit by the change.

Would that we could present a faithful picture of
the reign of Louis XIV. without finding ourselves perpetually compelled to sully our pages by a record of
heartless intrigues, which are so intimately involved
with the history of the time as to enforce even detailed mention.   To Mary de Mancini Louis XIV. was
indebted for his first intellectual ambition; Madem-

oiselle de la Vallière had taught him the real value of a devoted heart, and Madame de Montespan was about to impart to him the still more important secret of self-government.

When Louis succeeded in overcoming the resistance of La Vallière he was still young, and loved with a respectful and timid passion, which, constituted as he was, he afterwards exchanged towards his mistresses for the same arrogant and disdainful domination that he exhibited towards his subjects, and which a modest submission, like that of the unfortunate favourite whom we have seen the heroine of the fêtes of Versailles and St. Cloud, only tended to augment. He required, in order to contend with and overcome his self-love, a character as haughty and as imperious as his own; and he found what he needed in the beautiful, intellectual, but unprincipled and self-centred Marquise de Montespan.

CHAPTER IX

F RANCES ATHENAÏS DE ROCHECHOU-
ART DE MORTEMAR,* whom we have

* "The antiquity of the family of Montemar is registered in its
name, since the genealogists affirm that a noble who accompanied
Godfrey de Bouillon in his crusade obtained, as his share of the conquest, that portion of the Syria bordering upon the Dead Sea (*Mer-
morte*). Thence the name of *Mortimer* in England, and of *Mortemar*
in France."—*Louis XIV. et son Siècle.*

already introduced to our readers as one of the
companions of La Vallière, when, in the park of
Fontainebleau she betrayed her secret passion
for the King, and who was at that time Mademoiselle de Tonnay-Charente, had obtained, through
the interest of the Duchess of Navailles, an appointment as Lady of the Palace to the Infanta-
Queen, and by her superb beauty and brilliant wit
soon attracted the attention of the whole Court; but
this homage, flattering as it was, did not suffice to the
ambition of Mademoiselle de Tonnay-Charente, so
long as the King continued insensible to her attractions; and as he was constantly absorbed by her old
companion, La Vallière, she could devise no better
method of directing his attention to herself than by
exhibiting an extraordinary affection for the favourite.
She saw at a glance that the timid, tranquil, and unobtrusive affection of La Vallière was unaccompanied by
any mental exertion; and that, satisfied with the mere
fact of looking at and listening to the King, she was
incapable of amusing him in a moment of tedium, or
of assisting him in a season of difficulty. Resolute in
her determination never to be involved in any political
cabal, to solicit favours either for herself or others, or
to parade the triumph of her fault by making herself
conspicuous in the Court circle, she was ignorant of
all the graceful gossip in which Louis, in his private
hours, delighted to indulge. Absorbed in her affection for her Royal lover and his children, she was careless of literature and ignorant of art. In short, she
lived in her own little world of devotion and remorse,
and often met the Monarch with tears, which banished

the smile from his lips and chilled the ardour of his greeting.

Athenaïs de Mortemar felt her advantage, and profited by it to the utmost; and this constant contact ere long produced its effect. The King was struck by the affectionate devotion which she exhibited to her friend, the amiable zeal with which she superintended even the details of her toilet, and the ready wit with which she furnished her at every crisis with both words and ideas. His visits to La Vallière became more agreeable when he found that the high spirits of the handsome lady of the palace relieved him from the annoyance of a repentance which wounded his self-love, by imparting a portion of their buoyancy to his gentle mistress; and the "wit of the Mortemars" which had passed into a proverb not likely to be negatived in the person of Mademoiselle de Tonnay-Charente, proved an agreeable episode in his communion with his acknowledged favourite, for which he felt by no means disposed to be ungrateful.

Thus were things situated when the subtile beauty was compelled by her family to accept the hand of the Marquis de Montespan,* having, as she herself acknowledged, already bestowed her affections elsewhere.

During the first months of their union the Marquis expressed considerable satisfaction at her high station, and extreme popularity at Court; but, by his violent and unconcealed disgust at the attachment existing between the King and La Vallière, forewarned her of the little indulgence which she might anticipate at his

---

* Henry Louis de Pardaillan de Gondrin, Marquis de Montespan, of an illustrious family of Gascony.

hands should she be betrayed into any levity likely to dishonour his name. It is probable, however, that ere long he became weary of seeing his wife devoted to vanity and pleasure, and of the restraint imposed by her official duties; for, on succeeding to an inheritance in Provence, he urged her strongly to obtain leave to accompany him when he went to take possession of the property.

Madame de Montespan, however, young, beautiful, and admired, and, moreover, not sufficiently attached to her husband to make any sacrifice to his wishes when they interfered so fatally with her own private views, instantly made a pretext of her position, and pleaded with great earnestness the duty which she owed to her Royal mistress; suggesting that he should dispose of the estate to some member of his family, and reside entirely in the neighbourhood of the Court in which she aspired to shine.

Unable to prevail, and angered by her resistance, the Marquis at length resolved to leave Paris alone; and having, on his arrival at his new property, found everything greatly dilapidated, he applied all his energies to its improvement—still writing, however, from time to time, to urge the Marquise to join him. His entreaties and expostulations were of no avail. Madame de Montespan had become satisfied that the King began to feel pleasure in her society, and she resolved not to quit the Court.

While this new intrigue was thus commencing, Louis XIV., who had never for a moment lost sight of his Spanish interests, began to make preparations for a campaign. He had no apprehension as regarded the result of this contemplated war; for he was enabled to place himself at the head of thirty-five thousand men —to despatch eight thousand to Dunkirk, which, as well as Mardik, the needy and prodigal Charles II. had sold to him for five millions of livres—and to march four thousand troops upon Luxembourg. Well aware of the importance of Dunkirk, so rashly ceded and so eagerly acquired, the French King had at once employed thirty thousand men upon the works, and fortified the city on all sides. Between the town and the citadel a basin had been dug, capable of containing thirty vessels of war; and Dunkirk was no sooner beyond the power of the English than even their improvident Monarch himself was compelled to feel that his cupidity had raised him up a formidable enemy.

Moreover, not content with his internal resources, but anxious also to weaken the hands of his adversary, Louis made an alliance with Portugal and the United Provinces, who saw with misgiving a bigoted and superstitious nation so close upon their frontiers; while Turenne was to act as General of the army, and Colbert had spared no exertion to enable the State to support without injury the expenses of the war.

Louvois, the new War Minister, had, on his side, made extraordinary preparations for the campaign. Stores of every description were distributed along the frontier, and the rigid discipline which he had introduced, and enforced by his inflexible austerity, kept every officer to his post; while the presence of a young King, the idol of his army. was well calculated to reconcile them to increased stringency of their duties.

Military advancement began from that period, in France, to be more certainly secured by merit than by birth ; and services, instead of ancestors, were counted —a circumstance hitherto unprecedented, but most effective upon the spirit of the troops.

Such a campaign could scarcely with propriety be termed a war ; for on one side there was, as we have seen, an ambitious Monarch, an able General, and a zealous Minister ; a large body of the best soldiers in Europe, animated by a new and honourable hope ; and two allies ready to play their part in the game of conquest, whenever their services might be required against the ill-defended province of a kingdom, ruined in its resources and rent with feuds. On the other hand, there was a widowed Queen, whose timid and feeble rule left the Monarchy weak and defenceless, and whose Prime Minister was her confessor, a German Jesuit, called Father Nitard, a man perfectly able to subjugate the will of a penitent, but utterly incapable of governing a State—full of ambition and arrogance, but totally devoid of the necessary qualities calculated to render him eminent either as a Minister or a Priest. Even before his appointment to the high office for which he was subsequently indebted to the weakness of the widow of Philip IV., he had the insolence to exclaim to the Duke of Lerma, who was reproaching him with his assumption, and reminding him of the deference due to his own rank :

" It is you who owe respect to me ; I who have every day your God in my hands and your Queen at my feet."

And yet this presumptuous Priest, who was so ready

to assert himself even thus blasphemously and disloy-
ally, left the treasury without funds, the fortifications
all over the country in a state of ruin, the ports without shipping, and the army undisciplined, unpaid, ill-
officered, and utterly incapable of contending with
such troops as were about to be brought against them;
while the frontiers of Flemish Spain were almost desti-
tute alike of fortresses and of garrisons.

Louis XIV. was so well aware of these facts, that he
caused himself to be accompanied throughout the
campaign by all the ladies of the Court, and the
expedition was a mere series of easy triumphs and
elegant revel. Luxury of every description was thus
introduced into the army at the same period as the
rigid discipline to which we have already alluded.
Marshal Turenne had for years used nothing but iron
dishes at his table; and the Marquis d'Humières was
the first who, at the siege of Arras, in 1658, had displayed a service of plate, and introduced the refinement of complicated cookery. In the campaign of
1667, however, when Louis XIV. paraded all the magnificence of his Court amid the turmoil of a camp,
every individual strove to outvie his neighbour in
splendour and expense.

The progress of the French was one continued
triumph. Louis presented himself before Charleroi,
and entered the city as he would have entered Paris;
Ath and Tournay were taken in two days; Furnes,
Armentières, and Courtrai held out no better; he
descended the trench in person before Douai, and took
it the next day; * but the most remarkable event of the

* Le Siècle de Louis XIV.

campaign was the siege of Lille, on which occasion the
Count of Brouai, its Governor, sent to ask him which
quarter of the camp he occupied, in order that he might
not fire upon it. His answer was, " All quarters."

When the action took place he exposed himself considerably, and a page of the Royal stable was killed
immediately behind him in the trench; upon which a
soldier, alarmed at his danger, seized him abruptly by
the arm and dragged him back, exclaiming, " This is
no place for you ! " As the King hesitated, startled
by the words and action of the trooper, the veteran
Marquis de Charost * snatched off his plumed hat,
which was too remarkable, and placed his own upon
the head of the King, whispering as he did so, " Sire,
the wine is drawn, and it must be drank." The young
Monarch heard and appreciated the admonition, remained in the trench, and felt grateful to him throughout his life for the timely lesson.

Every day M. de Brouai, finding that there was no
ice in the camp, sent a given quantity to the King,
who, on one occasion, desired the gentleman by whom
it was brought to request the Governor, if he could
conveniently do so, to increase the supply.

" Sire," answered the Spaniard, bowing gravely, " he
is chary of it, because he hopes that the siege will be of
long duration, and he is apprehensive that your Majesty

---

* Charost was celebrated for his courage in the field, and had greatly
distinguished himself during the wars of Henry IV. He had been the
protégé of Richelieu, who made him captain of the body-guard; and
Mazarin, who affected to protect all who were the favourites of his predecessor, became his friend, and recommended him first to the Queen-
mother, and subsequently to the King. His son married the only
daughter of Fouquet by his first marriage, but even the disgrace of
that Minister never diminished the Court favour of the Charosts.

may ultimately suffer from the deprivation." And he made a second profound bow.

" Tell M. de Brouai," exclaimed the Marquis de Charost, " not to act as the Governor of Douai did, who surrendered himself like a rogue."

" Are you mad, Charost ? " asked the King.

" Not at all, sire," answered the veteran, composedly; " for M. de Brouai is my cousin." *

The hope of the brave veteran was realised, as Lille held out for nine days before it capitulated, although the Spaniards had only eight thousand men to oppose to the victorious troops of Louis; and the vanguard of even this little army was cut to pieces by the Marquis de Créqui, while the main body took refuge under the walls of Brussels and Mons, leaving the French King master of the field without any further engagement.

The rapidity of these conquests spread alarm in Brussels, whose inhabitants hastened to transport all their property to Antwerp, uncertain whether Louis would not terminate the campaign by making himself master of the whole of Flanders, which it is extremely probable he might have done, had his army been strong enough to enable him to garrison the towns which were ready to open their gates. He was, however, advised by Louvois rather to leave large bodies of troops in the cities already taken, and to fortify them in an efficient manner; to which he acceded, confiding the direction of the works to Vauban,† one of those

---

* Louis XIV., sa Cour, et le Régent.

† Sebastian Leprestre de Vauban, a celebrated engineer, was born at St. Léger de Foucheret, in the department of the Nièvre in 1633, and in his seventeenth year entered the regiment of Condé, to whose fortunes he attached himself. He was soon distinguished for his

wonderful men of genius who were the best illustrations of his reign; and this arrangement completed, the victorious Monarch hastened to return to his Capital, to enjoy the acclamations of the people, the adoration of the courtiers, and the festivities of the Court.

The Flemish campaign had, however, other results beside those which we have already recapitulated. The King had been brought into frequent contact with Madame de Montespan both at Versailles and St. Germain; but during the journey to the frontier she had still better opportunities of ingratiating herself; nor had she been less careful to conciliate the favour of the queen, of which she availed herself to undermine her partiality for La Vallière so successfully, that the latter was subjected to constant affronts which reached their culminating point on an occasion when she chanced to be somewhat late in joining the dinner-party, and found, on entering the room, that the Queen had so filled the table that no seat remained unoccupied; upon which she immediately retired to her apartments, where she learned that her Majesty had expressly forbidden that refreshments should be furnished to her, a command which was, however, disobeyed.*

talents in engineering, and greatly assisted in the sieges of Stenai, Clermont, Landrecies, Condé, Valenciennes, Montmédi, Ypres, Gravelines, and Oudenarde. He directed that of the fortress of Luxembourg in 1683. Appointed Marshal of France in 1703, Commissary-General of fortifications, and Governor of Lille; he died in 1717. Vauban restored 300 ancient fortresses, and constructed thirty-three new ones; conducted fifty-three sieges, and was in more than 140 engagements. He left behind him several writings; among others, a *Treaty on the Attack and Defence of Fortified Cities*, a work on the *Royal Tythe*, and *Hours of Idleness*, a literary miscellany.

* Le Siècle de Louis XIV.]

The mortification she had experienced, nevertheless, determined Madame de la Vallière to return at once to Compiègne, where she had left Madame Colbert and her children, and thence to proceed to Versailles to await the conclusion of the campaign; and she had actually taken leave of the Queen, after writing to inform the King of her intention, and made a day's journey towards the Capital, when a letter from her Royal lover, reproaching her with her precipitation, at once caused her to retrace her steps.

It was late in the evening when she was overtaken by the messenger, and a long day's journey separated her from the King; she therefore resolved to travel all night, in order to overtake the Court by dawn, and just as the sun rose she arrived at Guise.

On inquiring for the Queen, she found, however, that she had left the town an hour previously; and terrified lest the Royal pair should meet before she had secured an opportunity of explaining to Louis the reasons which had induced her abrupt departure, she desired her attendants to increase their speed, and to overtake the army at any risk.

She was obeyed; but as the carriage was advancing through a gorge of the mountain, she was unable to calculate her progress, until, arriving in a spot that commanded the plain, she suddenly perceived the whole body of the army with a small detached group a short distance in advance, and at once recognised the personal staff of the King, from which she was only separated by a newly-ploughed field encumbered with stones.

As her coachman hesitated to advance, fearing an

accident, she repeated her commands, and ere long was in considerable peril from the severe shocks occasioned to her equipage by the masses of rock that were scattered in every direction; but she, nevertheless, persisted in advancing, as she found that she was gaining ground upon the Queen, who followed the beaten road. She had, however, scarcely time to distinguish the figure of the King, when a violent crash warned her that her carriage had given way, and in another instant it was overturned. A sharp pain in her arm convinced her that she had sustained a severe hurt; but she was too anxious to justify herself to heed the accident, and she was no sooner disengaged from the fallen vehicle than she insisted that it should be raised, in order that she might pursue her journey. With some difficulty this was accomplished, and she soon reached the King, which she had no sooner done than, with an exclamation of delight, she showed herself at the window.

"What! before the Queen!" said Louis, so soon as he had recognised the adventurous traveller; and with these few but reproachful words, he turned the head of his horse, and moved forward towards the advancing equipages of the Royal retinue.

Maria Theresa, who had witnessed the whole proceeding, was pale with anger, and was about to send one of her attendants to arrest La Vallière on the spot, when her ladies entreated her to desist, representing the probable consequences which would ensue to herself from such a measure; and she was at length appeased by the blame which they liberally bestowed upon the insolent favourite, of which no one was more

lavish than Madame de Montespan, who wound up
her objurgation by exclaiming, " Heaven preserve me
from being the mistress of the King !   But if I were
so unfortunate I should never have the effrontery to
appear before the Queen."

Maria Theresa thanked her by a look of gratitude;
for she had never for a moment suspected the virtue,
and far less the rivalry of the Marchioness, who was
her almost constant companion, and who was accustomed to bear her company every evening while she
awaited the arrival of the King in her apartments.
Insensibly the Lady of the Palace acquired a habit of
lingering near her Royal mistress after his entrance,
and Louis, on his side, of including her in the conversation which ensued; and as she possessed, in an
eminent degree, the " wit of the Mortemars," and was
caustic, agreeable, full of anecdote, and an admirable
mimic, he soon acquired a marked taste for her society;
while the Queen, thoroughly deceived by her professions, and the fact that she even joined her in her
private devotions, encouraged her in her exertions to
amuse the Monarch, flattering herself that, by rendering her own circle more agreeable, she should ultimately succeed in weaning him from his passion for
La Vallière.

But to return to the perilous exploit of the Duchess.
The Queen, although she had permitted herself to be
dissuaded from giving any public sign of her displeasure, nevertheless returned the greeting of her Royal
Consort, when he reached her carriage, with such
marked coldness that he inquired its cause, when she
overwhelmed him with reproaches for having per-

mitted her to be subjected to such an affront as she had just experienced. Soon wearied by her complaints, the King, after a brief attempt to calm her anger, in which he was unsuccessful, withdrew his hat, and, after a cold but graceful salutation, galloped off in the direction of the troops; but in five minutes more he was beside the equipage of La Vallière, whom he found drowned in tears. Their reconciliation was the work of an instant; and, on ascertaining that she had experienced an accident, he ordered his surgeon to be immediately summoned, who soon discovered that the arm was injured, and must be instantly bound up.

The King remained to support the Duchess during the operation in a state of the most painful agitation, after which he himself accompanied her in a carriage to Guise, where he lodged her in the best house that the town afforded, and ordered M. Séguin not to leave her for a moment. A slight fever supervened; but on the morrow she was declared convalescent, and Louis, who had little sympathy for lingering indisposition in those about him, sent a carriage to convey her to the mass, and his own equerry to attend her. She consequently appeared with her wounded arm in a sling, and at the conclusion of the service the King insisted upon her resuming her place in the Queen's carriage.

In the interval the Royal pair had again met, and when Madame de la Vallière presented herself at the moment of departure, all the ladies by whom it was already occupied hastened to offer their places, not even excepting MADEMOISELLE, who was seated beside the Queen; nor did Maria Theresa herself fail to greet

her trembling rival with more than ordinary graciousness.   In the evening, as the supper was served,
Madame de la Vallière prepared to withdraw, but was
detained by the Queen herself, who motioned her to a
seat opposite her own, while the King exerted himself
to evince his satisfaction at what was taking place
about him.   On glancing round the table La Vallière
remarked that Madame de Montespan had not joined
the circle; nor was she the only individual who had
noticed her absence.   In the course of the evening
she, however, appeared, and was immediately besieged
with inquiries and reproaches, to which she pleaded a
violent headache; and, contrary to her usual custom,
instead of seeking to enliven the party by sallies of
wit or brilliant freaks of fancy, she assumed a melancholy demeanour which attracted the attention of the
King.

On one or two occasions she approached Madame
de la Vallière and conversed with her in an under-
tone; but the moment she saw the Monarch about to
join them, she moved away, and, eventually, she seated
herself at a card-table, and motioned her unsuspicious
rival to her side.   The King shortly afterwards followed, declaring that he would give her advice which
would insure her success; but she played wilfully
wrong; and, after having for a short time supported
his remonstrances, remarked that she saw his Majesty
wished her to leave the table, and that, as such was the
case, she would ask Madame de la Vallière to take her
cards, in order that the party might not be broken up,
which would displease the Queen; and, so saying, she
rose, gave her chair to the Duchess, and seated her-

self in the recess of a window. For a time the King continued his instructions to La Vallière, but with evident absence of mind; and, eventually, he followed the Marchioness, and stood conversing earnestly with her. Maria Theresa smiled; but it was far otherwise with the wretched Louise, who became suddenly conscious that her day of triumph was drawing to its close.

Another circumstance sufficed to assure her of the fact. The King had altered the arrangement of the apartments, and given to Madame de Montespan that which had previously been occupied by the Duchess of Montausier,* which was only separated from his own by a short staircase; and this change had no sooner been made than it was remarked that the Marchioness frequently quitted the Queen's card-table, or the drive, and retired to her room, and that the King disappeared at the same time and shut himself into his own.

But however prosperously the wily Marchioness might be conducting her intrigue, she was not without misgivings on the subject of her husband. His frequent and urgent letters broke in frightfully upon her dreams of ambition; and at length she received one in which he offered to pledge himself that if she would devote five or six years exclusively to his interests, he would then restore her, for the remainder of her life, to the gayeties of the Court. " Come and take a near view, my dear Athenais," it concluded, " of these

---

* Julia d'Angennes, first lady of honour to Anne of Austria, who in 1654 married Charles de St. Maure, Duke of Montausier, and was subsequently governess to the Dauphin.

stupendous Pyrenees, whose every ravine is a land-scape, and every valley an Eden.   To all these beauties yours is alone wanting; you will be here, like Diana, the divinity of these noble forests."

The flatteries of a husband had, however, unfortunately, no attraction for Madame de Montespan.   In reply to this urgent appeal she contented herself by asserting that his impatience and ill-humour made her wretched; and that, as five or six of her colleagues * were either sick or absent, it was impossible for her to abandon her post, but pledged her honour that in the autumn, on the return of the Court from Fontaine-bleau, she would immediately join him.

This compromise by no means satisfied the Marquis, who had already been apprised that she was endeav-ouring, under the mask of friendship for Madame de la Vallière, to attract the attention of the King; and he consequently wrote, coldly and imperatively, to in-form her of the extent of his knowledge, and to an-nounce his intention of returning to Paris, in order to ascertain the exact nature of her imprudence, which he threatened to expose, not only to her own family, but to the world; commanding her, at the same time, to confide her son to the guardianship of his messenger, that he might not become contaminated by contact with a mother who had thrown off all restraint; and adding, that on his arrival in the Capital, he would shut her up in a convent, if she had not previously in-trigued to send him to the Bastille.

The threat came, however, too late to produce the

* After the death of Anne of Austria Louis XIV. increased the number of ladies of the palace from six to eighteen.

desired effect upon the erring wife. She had already
secured a powerful protector; but it nevertheless
operated so greatly on her fears, that on the evening
of the day on which it reached her the King detected
her agitation, and insisted upon learning its cause.
Madame de Montespan replied by placing the letter in
his hand. The King changed colour as he read; and
then observed that their position was one of difficulty,
and exacted great precaution, but that he would take
care that no violence should be offered to her; and
advised her at once to give up her son, who " was useless, and perhaps inconvenient"; while the fact of
being deprived of his child might drive the Marquis to
some act of severity.

To this, however, Madame de Montespan would not
consent, declaring that she would sooner lose her life;
and her tears so moved the King that he ultimately
desired her to retain the boy near her, and he would
endeavour to obviate the consequences. The Marquis
redeemed his word. Ere long he arrived in Paris,
and cited his wife before the authorities of the Chatelet.
He addressed a firm and reproachful letter to the King,
and applied to the Pope for a *réclamation*, urging him
to authorise a divorce; but although he unweariedly
pursued his solicitations through three entire months,
his Holiness, fearful of offending Louis XIV., refused
to accede to his petition; and he no sooner became
convinced that he should not succeed than he assumed
the deepest mourning, hung the carriage entrance of
his house with black, and covered his servants and his
equipages with the same sable drapery. He then
ordered a funeral service to take place at the parish

church, to which he invited the whole town and neighbourhood, and publicly asserted that he had no longer
a wife; that Madame de Montespan had died of an
attack of levity and ambition; and even declared his
intention of contracting a second marriage at the termination of his year of widowhood.

This exhibition of contempt for the Marchioness, so
ludicrously displayed, greatly annoyed the King, who
could not shut his eyes to the fact that he was himself
involved in the ridicule which it excited. But fortunately for his self-love, the Marquis, having satisfied
his vengeance by this exposure of the intrigue, shortly
afterwards left France.

" Not being naturally of a bad disposition," says
Madame de Montespan, with great complaisance, after
having given the above detail, " I never would allow
M. de Louvois to send him to the Bastille. On the
contrary, I secretly paid his debts, which amounted to
more than fifty thousand crowns, very glad to do him
this service in return for the evil which he said of
me." *

It is a strange proof of the perverted feeling and
accommodating morality of the time, that although,
upon the evidence of his guilty wife, M. de Montespan
had left no measure untried to reclaim her, there is
nevertheless not one historian of the century who
does not seek to cast upon the forsaken husband the
odium of this revolting intrigue, and affect to say that,
from motives of base and sordid interest, he encouraged a crime which made his home desolate and induced him to forsake his country. We have faithfully

* Mémoires de Madame de Montespan.

quoted the account of the whole transaction from the words of Madame de Montespan herself, who cannot be suspected of exhibiting too great a partiality towards a man whom she had so greatly wronged, and consider all argument upon such a question as worse than supererogatory.

CHAPTER X

The Daughters of Gaston, Duke of Orleans—La Grande Mademoiselle—Mademoiselle de Valois, Duchess of Savoy—
Mademoiselle d'Orleans, Grand Duchess of Tuscany—Mademoiselle d'Alençon, Duchess of Guise—Letter of Madame
de Sévigné—Mademoiselle and the Duke of Lauzun; His
Portrait by St. Simon; His Court-Favour; His Advancement; His Indiscretion; His Insolence; His Imprisonment
in the Bastille; His Pardon—Mademoiselle Becomes Attached to Him—Reluctance of Lauzun—Mademoiselle Offers
Him Her Hand—Preliminaries—Interview of Louis XIV. and
Mademoiselle—The King Consents to Her Marriage with
Lauzun—Consternation of the Court—Donation by Mademoiselle—Louis XIV. Withdraws His Consent—Agony of
Mademoiselle—Submission of Lauzun—The Private Marriage
—New Arrest of Lauzun; His Ingratitude.

AND now we will glance for a moment at the family of Gaston, Duke of Orleans. MADEMOISELLE,
the sole heiress of all the fiefs of Orleans, and mistress
of an income of seven hundred thousand livres, who
had refused an Emperor, three reigning Monarchs,
Philip of France, and half a dozen sovereign Princes,
still remained unmarried, and was about, in her fortieth
year, to bow her pride before a passion as weak as it
was ill placed.

We have seen that this Princess had, in the first instance, peremptorily declined an alliance with the Duke

of Savoy, the only reason which she condescended to
adduce existing in the fact that Madame Royale, being
still alive, and a daughter of Henry IV., governing her
Duchy with unlimited authority, she should be compelled to yield her precedence, being herself only the
daughter of a younger son of France, who died in
banishment.

By no means driven to despair by his first failure,
the young Duke next asked the hand of her sister, Mademoiselle de Valois, as we have stated elsewhere; and
this Princess, whose disposition was all mildness and
obedience, at once complied with the wish of her
mother that she should accept so desirable an alliance.
The arrangement was, however, kept secret from MAD-
EMOISELLE, who was then in exile at St. Fargeau; and
who was, in her ignorance of what had taken place,
betrayed into her offer of marrying the once rejected
Duke as an alternative to avoid the alliance of the
King of Portugal.*

Mademoiselle de Valois, who was the handsomest
of the four sisters, did not long profit by the affection
of her new family, to whom she at once endeared herself by her amiable qualities, being cut off in the pride
of her beauty and the height of her happiness, in the
year 1664, nearly at the same period as Madame Royale and the Duchess of Parma—the high-minded
Princess Marguerite, who never recovered the mortification of her abortive journey to Lyons.

Mademoiselle d'Orleans, the elder sister of the second wife, was a fair and pretty woman, but indiscreet
in her conversation and undignified in her manner;

* Madame de Montespan.

who, at the period when her marriage was mooted with
the Prince Medicis, Grand Duke of Tuscany, had already bestowed her affections upon her maternal
cousin, Prince Charles of Lorraine—a fact of which
the King was cognisant, but would not countenance
the connection, as he secretly desired to possess himself of the principality of the suitor—and the Duchess-
Dowager consequently entreated her daughter to become Grand Duchess of Tuscany. The marriage
proved an unhappy one; which was attributable to the
fact that they were in constant dissension on the subject of etiquette, upon which they could never come
to a satisfactory understanding.

The younger of the three Princesses, Mademoiselle
d'Alençon, had she possessed more animation and intellect might have been esteemed a beauty; but she
was alike devoid of mind and of ambition, and her fine
black eyes were cold and expressionless. She had for
some time been the guest of MADEMOISELLE, by whose
assumption and arrogance she was rendered miserable,
when Mademoiselle de Guise,* the last representative
of the original House of Lorraine, whose immense
wealth secured to her a brilliant position in the world,
resolved, if possible, to secure her hand for her nephew,
the young Duke of Guise, then only seventeen years
of age; but in order to accomplish this object it was
necessary to obtain the consent of the King, who was
averse to the marriage, but by whom it was, nevertheless, ultimately permitted. The bridegroom, astonished at his good fortune, and totally devoid both of

* Sister of the celebrated Cardinal de Lorraine, Archbishop of
Rheims, etc.

pretension and ambition, could not suppress his surprise when the Monarch, instead of a dower, presented to the young Duchess a magnificent set of tapestry hangings and a service of enamelled gold, studded with jewels.

The unfortunate Duke had, however, little reason to congratulate himself upon his unequal marriage, for it had been arranged that Mademoiselle d'Alençon was to retain all her privileges as a member of the Royal house; and, consequently, M. de Guise could only occupy a folding-seat* in her presence. When she seated herself at table he presented her dinner-napkin, and when she was established in her armchair and had unfolded the *serviette*, M. de Guise meanwhile standing behind her, she ordered a plate to be placed before him, which was always ready upon the sideboard. This plate was then carried to the bottom of the table, where she desired him to sit down. Every other ceremony was observed with the same punctiliousness, and recommenced every day without any increase of condescension on the part of the wife; nor did he ever venture to address her save as "Your Royal Highness."

The Duchess became a widow in 1671, when the Duke was carried off by smallpox, leaving a son, who also died four years subsequently. Madame de Guise thenceforward grew extremely devout, and attached herself to the celebrated Abbot of la Trappe, whom she survived only a few months.†

---

* A *pliant* or folding-seat was a compromise of etiquette: more honourable than a stool, and less dignified than a chair.

† Mémoires de St. Simon.

MADEMOISELLE was, therefore, as we have already stated, the only one of the sisters who remained unmarried; and we cannot better announce the next phase of her career than in the sprightly words of Madame de Sévigné in a letter to M. de Coulanges, her cousin.

" I am about to inform you of the circumstance the most astonishing, the most surprising, the most miraculous, the most triumphant, the most bewildering, the most unheard-of, the most singular, the most extraordinary, the most incredible, the most unforeseen, the most immense, the most minute, the most rare, the most common, the most conspicuous, the most secret until to-day, the most brilliant, and the most enviable —in short, a circumstance of which there has been but one example throughout past centuries, and even that one is not precisely similar. . . . I cannot make up my mind to tell it—guess it—I will give you three guesses : *do you throw your tongue to the dogs ?* Well, then ! here it is. M. de Lauzun is to marry, on Sunday next, at the Louvre—guess who? I will give you four, I will give you ten, I will give you a hundred guesses. Madame de Coulanges says : It is by no means difficult to guess; it is to Madame de la Vallière : not at all, Madame. It is, then, to Mademoiselle de Retz : not at all, you are a mere country gentlewoman. The truth is, we are very dull, say you ; it is to Mademoiselle Colbert. Still less. It is, then, assuredly, Mademoiselle de Créqui : you are wrong again. It must end by my telling you : he marries on Sunday next, at the Louvre, by permission of the King, Mademoiselle, Mademoiselle de—Madem-

oiselle—guess the name: he marries Mademoiselle—
on my word, by my word, my solemn word!—
MADEMOISELLE, the great Mademoiselle; Mademoiselle, the daughter of the late MONSIEUR; Mademoiselle, the granddaughter of Henry IV.; Mademoiselle
d'Eu, Mademoiselle de Dombes, Mademoiselle de
Montpensier, Mademoiselle d'Orleans; Mademoiselle,
Cousin-german to the King; Mademoiselle, destined
to the throne; Mademoiselle, the only match in France
which was worthy of MONSIEUR. There is a fine subject of gossipry. If you exclaim, if you are beside
yourselves, if you say that we have fibbed, that it is
not true, that we are quizzing you, that it is a poor
jest, and a tame fancy enough; if, in short, you abuse
us, we shall consider that you are right; we should
have done as much to you. Adieu; the letters which
go by this post will show you if we tell the truth or
not."

This ejaculatory letter will prove the extent of the
astonishment felt by the patrician families of France
at the intelligence which Madame de Sévigné hastened
to impart to her family. It was even so: the punctilious, fastidious, arrogant, and self-worshipping MADEM-
OISELLE, after amusing herself by rejecting, during her
years of bloom and grace, half the Sovereign Princes
of Europe, had, indeed, in the autumn of her life, bestowed her unsolicited affections upon a mere handsome adventurer; and, what is still more extraordinary,
the haughty Louis XIV., imagining a parallel between
the attachment of his cousin for Lauzun and his own
for La Vallière, had actually suffered himself to be
persuaded to permit a marriage wholly without prec-

edent, and calculated to shock the prejudices of all the Royal and noble families throughout his kingdom.

We have already mentioned the presentation of M. de Péguilain to Louis XIV. by his uncle, the Duke of Grammont, and the immediate effect which he produced upon that Monarch.

Antonin Nompar de Caumont, Duke of Lauzun, born in 1632, arrived in Paris under the name of Marquis de Péguilain; and, according to St. Simon, was " a little beau, well made, with an open and intellectual countenance; full of ambition, whims, and fancies; envious of every one, never satisfied with anything; always anxious to exceed his limits; without any literary taste or knowledge; naturally irritable, misanthropical, and abrupt; very profuse in his habits; constitutionally ill-natured; eminently jealous; a warm friend, when he thought proper to be so, which was rare; a ready enemy even towards those who were indifferent towards him; clever in detecting defects, and in discovering and bestowing ridicule; a merciless quizzer; extremely and dangerously brave; a clever Courtier according to circumstances; haughty to insolence or pliable to servility; in short, to define his character in three words, as his actions have proved him, the boldest, the most dexterous, and the most cunning of men."

Such as he is here described, the crafty Marquis soon won upon the King, who required constant amusement, and found it in the conversation of this new favourite, for whom he raised a regiment of dragoons, appointing him shortly afterwards Adjutant-General, and finally Colonel-General of cavalry.

Some months subsequently, the Duke of Mazarin, having decided upon retiring from the Court, was anxious to dispose of his charge of Grand-master of the Artillery; and this fact had no sooner reached the ears of Lauzun than he applied to the King for the appointment, who promised it to him without difficulty, provided he kept his intention perfectly secret, telling him that it should be arranged on the day fixed for holding a Council of Finance. This day had no sooner arrived than Lauzun established himself in the ante-room through which Louis passed to the council-hall, and entered into conversation with Nyert, the first valet-de-chambre on duty, who inquired in a friendly manner the nature of his business. Lauzun, who now considered himself sure of the appointment, believed that he should secure the interest of this man by informing him of what was about to take place, and accordingly betrayed his secret; upon which Nyert offered his congratulations, drew out his watch, and perceiving, as he asserted, that he had still time to execute a pressing order given him by the King, which would not occupy more than five minutes, left the room, sprung up a private staircase which led to the study of Louvois, and briefly communicated to him the intelligence which he had just gained.

Lauzun was the friend of Colbert, and this fact alone sufficed to insure to him the enmity of Louvois, who, moreover, feared the influence of the reigning favourite in a charge operating so powerfully and interfering so closely with the War Department. He accordingly dismissed Nyert with warm thanks, begged him immediately to resume his post, and hastily gathering up a few papers to serve as his introduction, walked through the anteroom, where he found Lauzun and Nyert again conversing together. The latter affected extreme surprise at his appearance, and represented to him that the Council was still sitting; to which the Minister replied that he was compelled to enter, as he had pressing business with the King, and proceeded on his way.

When he entered Louis rose, and, retiring with him to the recess of a window, inquired the cause of his coming; to which he answered that he understood his Majesty was about to declare M. de Lauzun Grandmaster of the Artillery, who was awaiting the declaration of his appointment at the close of the Council; that he was quite aware of the power of the Sovereign to bestow his favours as he saw fit, but that he considered it his duty to venture to represent to his Majesty the incompatibility which existed between M. de Lauzun and himself; that his Majesty was aware of the haughty wilfulness of the former, who would inevitably make serious changes in the administration of the artillery without consulting any one; while that particular charge was so intimately connected with the War Department that it was vitally impossible for the service to be carried on, should there exist a declared misunderstanding between the Grand-master and the Secretary of State, as that misunderstanding would involve his Majesty in the annoyance of being every day importuned by their mutual claims, upon which he alone was competent to judge.

The King, greatly vexed to find that his secret had been discovered by the very individual from whom he had been most anxious to conceal it, reflected for a moment, and then saying " It is not yet done," turned away and resumed his seat at the Council.

When the members separated, Lauzun presented himself to the King as he passed out, and was unable even to catch his eye. Twenty times during the day he placed himself upon his path, but Louis never alluded to the appointment. At length, as he was assisting at the *petit coucher*, the Duke ventured to ask if his commission were signed; when the King answered coldly that it could not be done yet, but that he would think about it. Several days having, however, elapsed, without any further mention of the matter, Lauzun requested a private audience, and, after a few inconsequent remarks on both sides, the insolent favourite claimed the fulfilment of the Royal promise, in terms equally imperious and unbecoming. To this arrogant appeal Louis replied that he considered his promise to be annulled, inasmuch as it had been made only on a condition of secrecy on his own part, which he had violated; when Lauzun, moving a few paces aside, turned his back upon the King, drew his sword, broke the blade across his knee, and swore that he would never again serve a Prince who was capable of so *foully* falsifying his word.

The eye of the King flamed for an instant; but as he raised his cane to strike the audacious courtier, a feeling of what was due to his own dignity caused him to throw it through the window near which he stood, as he said, sternly, " I should be sorry to strike a man of quality," and forthwith left the room.*

Lauzun felt his error when it was too late. The

* Mémoires de St. Simon.

next day he was an inmate of the Bastille, and the artillery was given to the Count of Lude.*

While a prisoner, the Duke committed for awhile a thousand follies, suffered his beard to grow, and talked like a madman; but soon wearying of his incarceration, he became more rational, and accused himself of his downfall, declaring that the King had been more lenient than he deserved, and that he regretted nothing save the Royal favour, although his fortunes were utterly marred.

As he anticipated, all these loyal expressions were reported to the Sovereign, who, flattered by such extraordinary devotion to his person, and anxious to regain the companionship which he had lost, caused it to be intimated to him that, conciliated by his repentance, his Majesty was willing to bestow upon him the Captaincy of the Guards; but, contrary to the expectations of Louis, the favourite, upon learning this sudden and unhoped-for revolution in the Royal mind, flattered himself that he was indispensable, and might make better terms; and the result of this conviction was a respectful but firm refusal to accept the appointment. The King was not, however, to be denied; the proposition was repeated, and eventually Lauzun, with an affected reluctance which savoured of condescension, agreed to consent to the wishes of the Sovereign. He accordingly passed from the Bastille to the most confidential post at Court, paid his respects to the King, took the oath, and found himself more than ever popular at Court.†

---

* Afterwards Duke of Lude.
† Lauzun was appointed Captain of the Guard in 1669. (*Dangeau.*)

It was at this period that he first attracted the attention of MADEMOISELLE, who, after giving a very partial and garbled account of the transaction which we have just narrated, declares that he performed his duties with a noble, graceful, and easy demeanour that gratified the King; and that, when she congratulated him upon his restoration to favour, he assured her he was quite conscious of the honour which she conferred upon him by thus evincing an interest in his fortunes. In short, the Princess confesses that she thenceforth began to look upon him as an extraordinary man, whose conversation was so agreeable that she sought opportunities of enjoying it, and discovered that he expressed himself in a manner unapproachable by any other person.† Indeed, her whole account of the advances which she made to the handsome courtier are inexpressibly amusing: his evident reluctance to involve himself with a mistress of forty years of age is shadowed out legibly, even while the deluded lady herself supposes it to be merely the awe inspired by her high birth and her personal attributes; and this inconvenient respect became at last so apparently unconquerable, that MADEMOISELLE was compelled not only to turn upon him all her " nods, becks, and wreathed smiles," but actually to hint to him that her hand was at his service. Thenceforward she encountered no opposition—his ambition was aroused—he remembered her rank, her wealth—and that her husband would become the cousin of the King of France—and the whole Court contained no other lover whose devotion could emulate that of the happy M. de Lauzun.

* Mémoires de Mademoiselle de Montpensier.

MADEMOISELLE, his senior by twelve or fourteen years, never imagined that he could love her from interested motives; for even conscious as she was both of the dignity of her rank and the value of her possessions, her vanity was more powerful than her reason; and, involved at the age of four-and-forty in a first passion, she obeyed its dictates as though she were still in the bloom of her youth and beauty, and forgot that other eyes must detect a change to which she continued wilfully blind.

Lauzun, whose numerous irregularities revenged him on the follies of his elderly mistress, encouraged her in her weakness—affecting the languishing glances and lover-like demonstrations exacted by her folly; and their attachment, once reciprocally declared, drew from her in their private conversation a detailed account of her possessions, which she revealed to him, even to the value of her plate and jewels. This done, the passion of the wily courtier reached its culminating point, for, by careful calculation, he ascertained that she was the mistress of at least forty millions. Having satisfied himself on this point, he next proceeded to enquire what would be his own position, should the King be induced to ratify their marriage, and if he should be elevated to the rank of a Prince. This, however, she frankly told him that she had not sufficient influence to accomplish, but that she would make him Duke of Montpensier, with an independent income of five hundred thousand livres. Then he desired to know if their united escutcheon would bear the coronet of the husband or the crown of the wife; to which she answered that, as she should not change her name, she could not change her shield, and that her armorial bearing must remain entire, supported by the crown with its *fleur-de-lis*. The next inquiry was whether their children should be Princes *de facto;* to which she declared that she saw no impediment; and finally, if there was a probability of his being ultimately raised to the rank of Prince, and recognised as a *highness* from the signing of the contract?

This last inquiry plunged MADEMOISELLE into a train of uneasy reflection; for, although blinded by her passion and misled by her vanity, she did not discover the supreme egotism of her lover, but rather rejoiced to find him punctilious upon points which were so important to herself and so precious in her own estimation, she was suddenly aroused to a serious doubt of the acquiescence of the King in such unprecedented arrangements; but as she was not easily induced to yield any point upon which she had resolved, and that in the present case she believed the whole happiness of her future life to be involved in her marriage with her lover, she determined at once to remove her doubts by a personal interview with the King. She accordingly ordered her equipage and her equerries; and having taken up her gloves and fan from the table, bade a hasty farewell to the anxious Lauzun, and drove to the Louvre.

The astonishment of Louis XIV. was unbounded. He reminded her of the thrones she had rejected; of the fact that she had entered her forty-fifth year; he endeavoured to make her sensible of the absurdity of her attachment; he essayed alike remonstrances and ridicule; but MADEMOISELLE was not to be repulsed; and ultimately, annoyed and even disgusted by her

pertinacity, he desired her, as she was resolved to commit so great a folly, and was quite old enough to judge
for herself, to rid him at once of her tears, and sighs,
and to do as she pleased.*

It must not, however, be supposed, that a Monarch
like Louis XIV. conceded so extreme a point as this
to the absurd demonstrations of an elderly coquette,
and thus compromised his own dignity by a weakness
which was unworthy of him, for such was far from
being the case. The lamentations of MADEMOISELLE
were so lengthy that they afforded him ample time for
reflection; and there can be no doubt but he became,
ere long, conscious that it might be more consonant to
his own interests to permit the marriage than to persist
in his opposition. MADEMOISELLE was the sole remain
of the once formidable party of the Fronde, and was
even yet reluctant to forget her past triumphs; by
marrying a Prince of the Blood she would retain at
least a reflection of her former importance, while in
becoming the wife of an obscure individual like
Lauzun, the richest heiress in France would descend
from her pedestal, and figure merely as a simple gentlewoman; and thus, by suffering a reluctant consent to
be wrung from him, he would rid himself of a troublesome and arrogant adversary.

On the morrow, therefore, the marriage was publicly
announced; on the following day MADEMOISELLE and
her betrothed received congratulatory visits from all
the Court; and on that which ensued the Princess, for
the purpose of investing M. de Lauzun with the titles
and honours requisite to adorn their contract, made

* Mémoires de Madame de Montespan.

him a formal donation of four Duchies—the Countship of Eu, the first Peerage in France, giving precedence of all other Peers; the Duchy of Montpensier, of which he immediately assumed the name; the Duchy of St. Fargeau; and the Duchy of Châtellerault—the whole estimated at twenty-two millions.

Nothing then remained save to sign the contract, to which it was anticipated that the King would append his name on the ensuing morning; but in the course of the day the Queen herself, who seldom ventured to give an opinion upon any transaction in which she was not personally involved, spoke indignantly against the alliance; while *Monsieur* declared that he would attend the marriage, if such were the will of his Majesty, but that on leaving the church he would blow out the brains of the bridegroom.* Hence the King passed into the apartments of Madame de Montespan, who informed him of the extravagant donation of the Princess; and this fact sufficed to irritate him beyond all bounds. He immediately summoned both MADEMOISELLE and Lauzun to attend him, and then, in the presence of the Prince de Condé, he declared, without preface or apology, that he absolutely forbade them to think any further of their marriage. The suitor received this order with all the submission and respect which could be anticipated; but MADEMOISELLE threw herself into an agony of grief, and besought Louis, upon her knees, to revoke a sentence which condemned her to a life of misery. Her entreaties were, however, unavailing; the King was inexorable, and she left his presence drowned in tears, and careless of concealing her despair.

* Mémoires du Marquis de la Fare.

Nothing could exhibit the overweening and egotistical vanity of Lauzun more fully than this failure, which was produced by his having delayed his marriage for a week, in order to prepare new liveries, to form an immense establishment, to secure magnificent attire, and to appear at the ceremony with all the splendour of a Royal personage—an imprudence which gave his enemies time to work upon the mind of the King, and thus induced his defeat; while the resignation with which he received the Royal command to forego his ambitious hopes astonished and confounded all who were aware of the arrogance and impetuosity of his character. But ere long it was ascertained that, having secured the services of a needy priest by a large bribe, he had accomplished his marriage with the infatuated Princess in secret—a fact of which the King no sooner became cognisant than he caused him to be arrested and conveyed to the fortress of Pignerol, where, while MADEMOISELLE was consuming her days in an uncontrolled grief that soon destroyed every trace of the good looks upon which she still prided herself, and lamenting to every one by whom she was approached her cruel separation from " her dear and tender friend, the prisoner," the Duke himself was committing every description of excess of which his position was susceptible, and dissipating in gaming and the most inane frivolities the immense sums of money secretly conveyed to him by the Princess; and whenever he found his funds exhausted, consoling himself by saying to his friends, " The old woman will send us a fresh supply." *

* Mémoires de Madame de Montespan.

CHAPTER XI

WE have, however, anticipated the stream of our
narrative, in order not to interrupt the history
of this extraordinary attachment; for great and melancholy events occurred at Court before it reached the
climax we have described.

The Duke of Beaufort, Grand-Admiral of France,
who had been sent by Louis XIV. to succour Candia,
which was besieged by the Turks, had found the whole
island, with the exception of the capital, in possession
of the enemy; and an attack was resolved upon at
daybreak on the 25th of June, which surprised the
Moslem troops in their sleep, and compelled them to a

confused retreat, that appeared to secure the triumph
of the Christian forces; but as they retired, they contrived to fire several barrels of powder, of which the
explosion caused so great a panic among the French
soldiery, that, despite all the efforts of their leaders,
they, in their turn, abandoned themselves to flight;
when M. de Beaufort, enraged at their cowardice,
boldly placed himself at the head of a small party of
gentlemen who still remained beside him, and dashed
furiously into the Turkish ranks, by which he was immediately inclosed, and not even his body was ever
again seen.

Meanwhile Madame de la Vallière had become a
constant guest in the circle of the Queen, where the
misunderstandings which constantly took place between
herself and Madame de Montespan were as constantly
reconciled by the intervention of the King, and were
rendered less serious by the ignorance in which the
former yet remained of the extent of the attachment
that really subsisted between her Royal lover and her
former friend, the birth of the Duke of Maine * being
still a profound secret from all the Court.

The treaty of Aix-la-Chapelle had awakened the
misgivings of the Dutch, who could not see without
uneasiness the approach of so dangerous a neighbour
as Louis XIV.; nor was their alarm causeless, for the
French King had become weary of a peace which
rendered nugatory all the preparations that he had
made for carrying out a prosperous war. Both ex-
ternally and internally his kingdom had acquired a

---

* Louis Augustus de Bourbon, the natural son of the King and
Madame de Montespan, was born on the 31st of March, 1670.

strength and a brilliancy which had been hitherto unprecedented. The seaports, previously dilapidated and deserted, were surrounded by defences, covered with well-manned vessels, and occupied by nearly sixty ships of large tonnage, capable of being appropriated as men-of-war. New colonies, protected by the French flag, were emigrating to America, the East Indies, and the coast of Africa; and notwithstanding this drain upon the population, immense edifices were in progress of erection under the eyes of the King, which occupied thousands of individuals; the interior of the Court and the Capital displayed the progress of the more refined arts; literature flourished; and taste and splendour were superseding the ruder and less sumptuous habits of former ages.

At the period of *Monsieur's* marriage, the King had exerted all his generosity in order to establish his household, and to augment his income in a manner worthy of his exalted rank, and calculated to satisfy his utmost ambition; nor is it probable that the Prince, whose greatest ambition was pleasure and costly apparel, would have advanced any further claim upon the Royal munificence, had he not been instigated to do so by his two handsome, but ill-selected favourites, the Chevalier de Lorraine * and the Chevalier de Rémecourt, who, anxious to build up their own fortunes upon those of their too-indulgent master, suggested to him the necessity of self-assertion, and the weakness of remaining the passive recipient of his brother's favours.

Thus urged, *Monsieur* commenced by demanding

* Of the branch of Armagna.

the government of a province, which was refused by
the King, who asserted that these governments could
not be given to a brother of the reigning Monarch
without involving a risk of civil war, as in the case of
Gaston of Orleans, who had exerted his authority to
levy both men and money in order to oppose the
Crown; and this reply was accompanied by an intimation that the Prince would do well in future to
silence the evil advisers who prompted him to such
mistaken claims.

Monsieur, somewhat disconcerted, declared that he
had received no such instigation, but that he had
acted solely on his own judgment.

Louis, however, remained incredulous; and inquired whether it was also his own judgment that had
led him to insist on a seat in the Privy Council,
which he had since lost by having betrayed the proceedings at which he had assisted?

The Prince, greatly annoyed by the rejoinder, but
unwilling to fail in every point, then declared that he
should be less mortified by the unexpected refusal to
which he had been subjected, if the King would accord to his wife, who was the daughter of a Crowned
Head, the privilege of occupying an armchair in the
saloons of the Queen; but here again he was fated to
prove unsuccessful; for Louis XIV. was less likely to
cede a point of etiquette than a measure of impolicy.

" That cannot be permitted," said the Monarch,
coldly; " and I beg of you not to persist in such a
request. It was not I who established these distinc-
tions; they existed long before you and myself. It is
to your interest that the dignity of the Crown should

neither be weakened nor encroached upon; and if, from Duke of Orleans, you should one day become King of France, I know you well enough to believe that this is a point upon which you would be inexorable. Before God, you and I are two beings precisely similar to our fellow-men; but before men, we appear as something extraordinary, superior, greater, and more perfect; and the day on which the people cast off this respect, and this voluntary veneration, by which alone Monarchy is upheld, they will see in us only their equals, suffering from the same evils, and subject to the same weaknesses as themselves; and this once accomplished, all illusion will be over. The laws, no longer sustained by a controlling power, will become black lines upon white paper; and your chair without arms, and my *fauteuil*, will be simply two pieces of furniture of equal importance. However, in order to gratify your wishes, I will appoint you to the government of any province that you may select, if you will, on your side, immediately concede in writing your consent to be put upon your trial as a mere subject, whenever there may exist any disturbance, of whatever description, in the province under your command."

Philip d'Orleans at once saw the incompatibility of such an arrangement, and withdrew his claim. But, lenient as the King had shown himself towards his brother, whose frivolous habits were ill-calculated to sustain his dignity in any position of authority, he was by no means inclined to exhibit equal forbearance towards the crafty and ambitious favourites by whom he had been urged to such unprecedented claims; and, accordingly, on an occasion in which an abbey in the appanage of *Monsieur* became vacant, to which he nominated the Chevalier de Lorraine, Louis refused to ratify the appointment; and commanded Le Tellier to inform the nominee that it was not his pleasure he should receive the abbey.

Monsieur, mortified to find his privileges thus invaded, and stung by the reproaches of the disappointed courtier, lost no time in appealing to the King, and inquiring the reason of his refusal to recognise his donation; but he received no other reply than that which had been given to the questions put by the favourite himself to the Secretary of State—it was not his pleasure.

Monsieur began to evince considerable irritation at this display of fraternal authority; but he was soon silenced by the Monarch, who once more calmly advised him to recollect himself, and to get rid of the dangerous counsellors by whom he was surrounded; upon which the Prince withdrew, but only to confide his annoyance to the already indignant Chevalier, who persisted in assuring him that he had induced this mortification by his own weakness, and that it behooved him to assume a higher tone with the King, who now took advantage of his timidity and submission.

The effect of this taunt ere long became so apparent in the altered demeanour of *Monsieur*, that Louis resolved to banish the insidious favourite; and he was accordingly arrested at the Chateauneuf, while closeted with the Prince, and conveyed to Pierre-Encise *—a measure

* A fortress situated on a rock above the right bank of the Saône at

which so enraged *Monsieur*, that he immediately retired to Villers-Cotterets,* declaring that he would
remain there until the Chevalier was set free. This
undignified proceeding only tended to increase the
displeasure of the King, who, after having despatched
M. Colbert to expostulate with him upon his conduct,
upon finding all remonstrance ineffectual, forwarded
an order for the transfer of the Chevalier de Lorraine
to the Chateau d'If, † with a prohibition against his
either writing or receiving letters, or being permitted
to converse with any one not on duty within the walls
of the fortress. This last act of severity produced the
desired effect: *Monsieur* returned, moody and dissatisfied, to Court; and the favourite was instructed to
take up his abode in Rome.

This amelioration, however, by no means restored
the temper of the Prince, who loudly accused *Madame*
of having caused the exile of the Chevalier; and their
dissensions became at length so serious, that Louis was
compelled to interfere, and to remind *Monsieur* that to
his reproaches on the subject of the Duke of Buckingham and the Count of Guiche, the Princess, should she
see fit to do so, might retort by still graver accusations.
The warning was not disregarded; but it was evident

Lyons, which was appropriated to the purposes of a state prison. It
was demolished in 1793.

* Capital of the department of the Aisne, seven and a half leagues
from Soissons. The town owed its origin to a Royal fortress which
was destroyed by the English, and subsequently reconstructed by
Francis I. Villers-Cotterets is situated in the midst of the forest of
Retz.

† A strong fortress, situated on the Marguerite Island, opposite
Cannes, celebrated as having been the prison of the man with the
Iron Mask, and Mirabeau.

that a great coldness had sprung up between the Royal couple, which neither attempted to conceal; nor did even the constant correspondence that he continued to entertain with his exiled favourite suffice to reconcile *Monsieur* to an absence which interfered with his amusements and embittered his temper.

It was at this period that Louis XIV., who had conceived the project of ultimately subjugating the whole of the Low Countries, resolved to commence his work of conquest by appropriating Holland. The conjuncture was a favourable one. The Dutch were masters of the high seas, but no power could be weaker upon land. Allied with Spain and England, and at peace with France, they relied with too much security upon the faith of treaties, and on the benefits of a widely-extended commerce. While their navy was unparalleled in Europe, their army was ill-disciplined and despicable; and upon this weakness Louis founded his strongest hope. But before he could with prudence commence the war, it was necessary to detach England from Holland; for so long as their alliance continued his success remained uncertain, while a rupture between the two states insured the ruin of the Low Countries.

The French King was, however, quite aware of the facility with which he could obtain the cooperation of Charles II., who had betrayed little indignation at the destruction of his vessels burned by the Dutch at the very mouth of the Thames—who had evinced no desire to avenge the aggression—who lived only for pleasure, and sought only to reign in indolent indulgence: but even to accomplish this he needed friends;

and Louis XIV., who at that period could raise money to any extent and for any purpose, well knew that he required only to proffer a large sum to the English Monarch, who was crippled by his Parliament, in order to induce him at once to embrace his own interests.*

❧ To insure the neutrality of Spain, the Marquis de Villars was despatched to Madrid, with instructions to impress upon the Spanish cabinet the advantage which must accrue to themselves from the depression of the Low Countries, their natural enemies; while a Princess of six-and-twenty was chosen by Louis XIV. as his plenipotentiary at the English Court.

❧ His ambassadress was *Madame*, the sister of Charles II., who, having consented to undertake the mission, was escorted to the coast by the Monarch and his whole Court, under the pretext of a journey to his recent conquests; and the pomp which was exhibited on this occasion exceeded all that had yet been witnessed, even during the reign of the pomp-loving Louis XIV. Thirty thousand men marched in the van and rear of the Royal party; some of them destined to reinforce the garrisons of the conquered country; others to work upon the fortifications; and others again to level the roads. The Queen was attended by all the most beautiful women of the Court. *Madame* shared her coach; and immediately behind them followed a second carriage, containing Madame de la Vallière and Madame de Montespan, who were even occasionally invited to take their places in the Royal equipage; while among the ladies selected to accompany *Madame*

* Louis XIV. et son Siècle.

to the English Court, the most beautiful was Louise Rénée de Panankoët, known as Mademoiselle de Kérouaile, who had also her secret instructions,* which she had accepted with as much alacrity as her Royal mistress.

The journey was, however, more magnificent than pleasurable. The Queen displayed a bitterness sufficiently excusable when it is remembered that she was compelled to submit to the constant companionship of the King's mistresses; while *Madame* suffered continually from the ill-humour of her husband, who could not forgive her for having left him in ignorance of the purpose of her visit to England; and who took that opportunity of reproaching her with all his real and imaginary injuries. The happiest of the party was MADEMOISELLE, who could contemplate from her carriage-window the graceful person of M. de Lauzun; who, in right of his post as a Captain of the Guard, was constantly in attendance near the Royal party.

Meanwhile all these arrangements had greatly excited the displeasure of *Monsieur;* but Louis affected not to perceive his annoyance, and the illustrious travellers had no sooner reached the coast than *Madame* and her magnificent suite embarked for England. The negotiation was perfectly successful. Charles was enchanted with the superb beauty of Mademoiselle de Kérouaile; and the offer of several millions, coupled with a promise that the handsome Lady of Honour should remain in England, at once induced the weak Monarch to accede to all that was asked of him, which he did the more readily from his hatred of the Dutch Calvinists.

---

* Subsequently Duchess of Portsmouth.

A treaty of alliance was consequently drawn up between the two Sovereigns, and the ratifications of this treaty were to be exchanged in the course of the following month.

The English King, attended by a large retinue, accompanied his Royal sister to Dover; whence she crossed to Calais, where she was received with all the honours due to a triumphant negotiator. The Court then returned to Paris, making a festival of every halt; and *Madame* established her Court at St. Cloud; while *Monsieur*, enchanted by the movement about him, and who could never long support a displeasure which, utterly devoid of dignity, always eventually evaporated in noise, began to accept with more complaisance the favours by which the King sought to compensate to him for his past annoyance; but he was far from extending the same indulgence to *Madame*, who had once more excited his indignation by accomplishing, during her visit to England, a reconciliation between her Royal brother and the Duke of Buckingham.

It was, consequently, matter of notoriety to the whole Court that *Monsieur* and *Madame* were once more alienated from each other, when a catastrophe, as melancholy as it was unforeseen, struck terror into every heart in France.

The Duchess of Orleans was at this period the most influential, and one of the most beautiful women at the French Court. Grateful for the effort which she had made to serve him, the King overwhelmed her with courtesy and consideration, and made her the object of every revel and the medium of every favour; while the Queen, who divided her time between her children, her devotions, and her Spanish attendants, was little more than a cipher in her own Court. Of timid and retiring habits, the constant gayety of the Royal circle wearied and alarmed her; and had not the King interfered, she would have willingly passed her life in her dressing-gown and slippers. On days of State ceremony, when she was compelled to appear in public, her temper was always ruffled; and she was to the last ill at ease in the sumptuous apparel exacted by her rank. Governed by the Señora Molina, her foster-sister, who soon assumed a consequence which her Royal mistress was far from emulating, she never acted save in accordance with her advice; and although incapable of injuring even those by whom she was herself injured, Maria Theresa was equally inert when she might have served those who were faithful to her interests; and thus it was rather duty than inclination which influenced all who formed her private circle.

Thus were things circumstanced when, on the 29th of June (1669), *Madame* rose at an early hour and visited *Monsieur* in his apartment; after which she conversed for a considerable time with Madame de la Fayette, to whom she declared herself to be in admirable health. On her return from the mass, the Princess went to the room of Mademoiselle d'Orleans, her daughter, who was then sitting for her picture, when she talked of her late visit to England, and enlivened the whole circle by her joyous spirits; and, on entering her own apartments, she asked for a cup of succoury-water, which she drank, and afterwards dined as usual.

The party then adjourned to the saloon of *Monsieur*, whose portrait was also in progress; and during the sitting, *Madame*, as she was frequently in the habit of doing, laid down upon the cushions and fell asleep.

During her slumber her face became so livid and ghastly that Madame de la Fayette, who was standing beside her, was struck by so extreme a change, and was just in the act of asking herself if it were possible that the mere absence of expression could work so complete an alteration in a countenance which she had always considered handsome, when the Princess suddenly awoke in such agony that even *Monsieur* became surprised and alarmed.

As she was retiring to her own room, *Madame* stopped for a moment, in the outer apartment, to converse with the Treasurer of the Duke, while *Monsieur* was preparing to start for Paris. On the staircase he, however, encountered the Duchess of Mecklenburg, and returned with her to the saloon; upon which *Madame*, leaving M. de Boisfrance, hastened to receive her illustrious guest. At that moment Madame de Gamache approached with a salver, containing another draught of succoury-water, in the enamelled cup from which the Princess was accustomed to drink, and a second glass for Madame de la Fayette, which were respectively presented to them by Mrs. Gordon, the waiting-woman of *Madame;* but, as the Princess still held the cup in one hand, she pressed the other to her side, exclaiming that she had so violent a spasm that she could scarcely draw her breath. She flushed painfully for an instant, and then turned very pale, exclaim-

ing, with a painful effort, " Take me away !   Take me
away !   I can support myself no longer."

Terrified and bewildered, Madame de la Fayette and
Madame de Gamache upheld the Princess, who with
considerable difficulty reached her chamber, where she
threw herself upon the bed, writhing like a person in
convulsions.   Her physician was summoned; but he
treated the attack lightly, declaring that, although
painful, it was utterly without importance, while
Madame continued to gasp out her conviction that she
was dying, and to entreat that her confessor might be
sent for.

As *Monsieur* knelt beside her bed, the suffering
Princess threw her arms about his neck, exclaiming,
" Alas ! sir, you have long ceased to love me; and you
are unjust, for I have never wronged you."

While all around her were in tears, she suddenly
raised herself upon her elbow, and declared her conviction that she had been poisoned by the succoury-
water, which she had drank during the day—that
probably some mistake had been made ; but that she
felt she had taken poison, and if they did not wish to
see her die they must administer an antidote.

Monsieur, who was still beside her when she made
this appalling assertion, betrayed neither agitation nor
embarrassment, as he directed that some of the water
should be given to a dog, in order that they might ascertain its effect; but Madame Desbordes, her first
femme-de-chambre, immediately interposed, declaring that it was not upon a dog that the experiment
should be made, but upon herself, as she had prepared
the beverage, into which no noxious ingredient had

been introduced, and that she considered it her duty to prove the truth of the assertion.

She accordingly poured out a glass of the succoury-water, and drank it on the instant.

Oil and other antidotes were then administered to *Madame*, which served only to excite fearful sickness, without, in any degree, alleviating the original symptoms; and the ⸢Princess became more and more anxious for the assistance of a priest, although her physician still maintained that her life was not in the slightest danger.

Before the arrival of the curate of St. Cloud, however, her pulse had become inaudible, and her extremities icy cold, and she was compelled to make her confession supported in the arms of one of her women. At the expiration of three hours, two additional physicians arrived, the one from Paris, and the other from Versailles ; but after a consultation with their colleague, they assured *Monsieur* that he need be under no apprehension, as they would answer for the recovery of the Princess.

At length the King arrived in his turn, accompanied by the Queen and the Countess of Soissons, and Louis was powerfully affected by the change which had taken place in the countenance of *Madame ;* while, for the first time, the physicians themselves declared that the evil symptoms were rapidly increasing. La Vallière, who followed the King, describes the appearance of the dying Princess as fearful. Her complexion was livid, her eyes burned with fever, her nose and lips had shrunk, and a cold dew covered her skin. Louis occupied a seat on one side of her bed, and

Monsieur stood on the other, weeping bitterly; all the attendants were drowned in tears, but were so bewildered that although the agonised invalid continually entreated them to apply other remedies which might at least mitigate her sufferings, they remained terror-stricken and helpless. It was in vain that both the King and *Monsieur* appealed to the physicians; they remained equally supine; but at length declared, that the failure of the pulse and the coldness of the extremities announced the presence of gangrene, and that it was time to summon the viaticum.

While things were in this state the English ambassador was announced, and he had scarcely entered the death-chamber when the Princess beckoned him to her side, and by great exertion conversed with him for a considerable time in English. This done, she declared herself ready to receive the viaticum; after which she took leave of her illustrious relatives, and recalled *Monsieur* to give him a last embrace.

The extreme unction was then administered, and during the ceremony M. de Condom* arrived, to whose eloquent and holy discourse she listened eagerly for a time, and then inquired if she might sleep. He was about, in consequence, to retire, when she motioned him to return, murmuring that she had deceived herself, for that the stupour under which she laboured was not drowsiness, but death. M. de Condom once more knelt beside her in earnest prayer; the crucifix escaped from her relaxed fingers, her lips moved convulsively for an instant—and all was over.

Only nine hours previously Henrietta of England

---

* Bossuet, afterwards Bishop of Meaux.

had been full of life, and loveliness, and hope—the idol of a Court, and the centre of the most brilliant circle in Europe; and now, as the tearful priest arose from his knees, the costly curtains of embroidered velvet were drawn round a cold, pale, motionless, and livid corpse.

This death was, however, not only terrible in itself, but rendered tenfold more awful by the rumours to which it gave birth. *Monsieur*, whose neglect of the Princess had been notorious, was an object of the darkest suspicion. It was remembered that the Chevalier de Lorraine, his especial favourite, had openly accused *Madame* as the instigator of his banishment, and dark hints were soon abroad, involving both the one and the other in the dreadful catastrophe which had just occurred.

When these rumours reached the King he could not conceal his consternation, and declared to Madame de Montespan that if he should ascertain that his brother was implicated in so black a crime, his head should fall upon the scaffold.

On a *post-mortem* examination of the body the presence of poison was discovered, and that of so corrosive a character, that the whole of the stomach was in a state of inflammation, and even partially destroyed;* a fact which was no sooner ascertained than the King summoned *Monsieur* to his presence, in order to compel him to acknowledge his share in the murder; and the extreme agitation which he evinced acted so painfully upon Louis, that, in the height of his horror and suspicion, he rushed upon his

* Mémoires de Madame de Montespan.

sword, when the Captain of the Guard, who was in the anteroom, entered hastily ; and the King, lowering the point of his weapon, his breast still panting with the violence of his emotion, demanded of the Prince a full and true confession of all that had occurred.

Monsieur, whose personal courage had never been contested, and whom the late scene had tended rather to restore to composure than to intimidate, clasped in his hand the insignia of the Holy Ghost, which he wore about his neck, and took a formal oath that he was innocent, both directly and indirectly, of the death of his wife ; upon which the King commanded him to withdraw, and retired to his cabinet to address a letter to the English Court, in which he stated that *Madame* had fallen a victim to a bilious fever ; while the same account was officially promulgated by the public papers, and the fact was attested by the certificates of five or six paid physicians.

Still painful misgivings haunted the mind of the King. He was, unhappily, too well aware that the Princess had died from poison ; and while he began to hope that *Monsieur* was innocent of any participation in the crime, he left no means untried to discover its actual authors. He soon ascertained that the succoury-water, which was the constant beverage of *Madame,* was kept in the closet of one of the antechambers of her apartment, in a china jug, near which stood another vessel full of pure water, in the event of the decoction proving too bitter. Nor did his discoveries terminate in so inconsequent a result as this ; for it was further revealed to him, that on the very day when the Princess died, a footman, suddenly entering the anteroom in question, found the Marquis d'Effiat, another favourite of *Monsieur*, busied at this closet, and hastily approaching him, demanded what he was doing there.

To this unceremonious question the Marquis had replied, with the greatest tranquillity, that he was aware of his intrusion, but that, being very much heated and extremely thirsty, and knowing that water was always kept there, he had been unable to resist his inclination to swallow a draught.

As the footman continued to grumble at the liberty which he had taken, M. d'Effiat, after repeating his apology, passed on to the saloon of the Princess, where he remained for above an hour, conversing in his usual manner with the other courtiers.

The King was no sooner cognisant of this circumstance than he became convinced that Purnon, the controller of the Princess's household, must have had some share in the catastrophe, and he accordingly determined to interrogate him. For this purpose he summoned M. de Brissac, who was then on guard, and ordered him to select half-a-dozen of his men upon whose courage and discretion he could place reliance, and, on the following morning, to seize Purnon before he left his room, and bring him to the Royal cabinet by a back staircase.

This order having been executed, Louis passed into the apartment, where the astonished and terror-stricken controller was awaiting his fate with much anxiety and considerable misgiving; and having dismissed M. de Brissac, and the valet by whom he was attended, in order to remain alone with the prisoner, the King ad-

vanced a few paces, and then, with his eyes sternly
fixed upon the pale countenance of Purnon, he sum-
moued him to reveal every circumstance relating to
the death of *Madame*, promising him a full pardon
should his details be proved true, and warning him
that his life would be the forfeit of the slightest
equivocation.

The controller, with mingled joy and apprehension,
pledged himself to tell all he knew, and that all was
fortunately well calculated to allay the worst apprehensions of the King.

He stated that *Madame* had, indeed, fallen a victim
to poison, sent from Rome for that purpose by the
Chevalier de Lorraine, through the medium of a country gentleman named Morel,* who was, however, unconscious of the nature of his commission, and by
whom it was delivered to the Marquis d' Effiat and the
Count of Beuvron, who were induced to second the
views of the Chevalier, from the fact that his absence
interfered greatly with their interests, and that they
felt there was no hope of his return during the lifetime
of *Madame*.

"But how," asked the King, doubtingly, "do you
account for the circumstance that the other persons
who drank of the same infusion with the Princess experienced no inconvenience?"

"Simply, sire," was the reply, "because the Marquis
d'Effiat had foreseen the possibility of such an occur-
rence, and had empoisoned, not the liquid, but the cup
in which it was contained, by rubbing it on the inside."

The King passed his hand across his eyes, and then,

---

* Mémoires de la Princesse Palatine.

assuming a sterner look and a more threatening attitude, he demanded, in a voice which he in vain endeavoured to render firm and cold,

" And *Monsieur*—was he aware of this foul plot?"

" No, sire," was the ready answer; " *Monsieur* cannot keep a secret, and we did not venture to confide in
him—he would have brought us to the scaffold."

The King drew a deep breath, as though he had
heaved a heavy weight from his breast.

" Will you swear to this?" he asked, after a pause.

" On my soul, sire." *

Louis asked no more; and, almost consoled for the
death of the unfortunate Princess by the conviction
of his brother's innocence, he recalled M. de Brissac,
and desired him to conduct M. Purnon to the gate of
the palace, and then to set him at liberty.

It would seem as though the King believed that he
owed some heavy compensation to *Monsieur* for the
frightful suspicion which he had entertained against
him; for it is certain that, after a short interval, the
Chevalier de Lorraine was recalled to Court, and, moreover, as St. Simon asserts, laden with benefits, despite
which fact he died so poor that, although his income
had amounted to a hundred thousand crowns, his
friends were compelled to bury him at their own
expense.

His death, moreover, was worthy of his life. On
the 7th of December, 1702, three years after that of
Madame, as he was standing at the Palais-Royal, talking to Madame de Maré, the governess of the Duke
of Orleans's children, and relating to her the particulars

* Mémoires du Duc de St. Simon.

of a debauch in which he had been engaged on the previous night, he was suddenly struck by apoplexy, became speechless, and shortly afterwards expired.*

The Court had forgotten the murder long before they were called upon to comment on the death of the murderer.

* Louis XIV. et son Siècle.

END OF VOLUME IV

Index

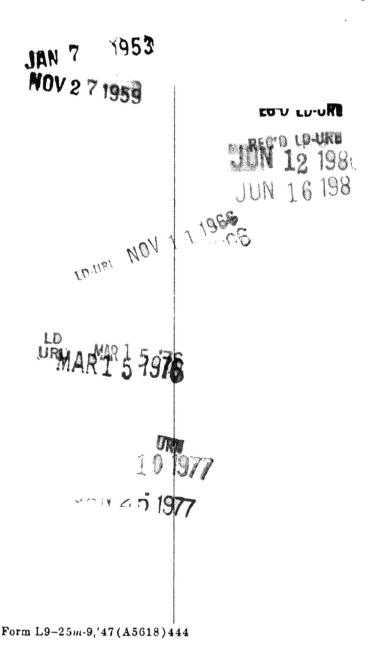

Lightning Source UK Ltd.
Milton Keynes UK
UKHW011301070119
335137UK00016B/1237/P